P9-CDL-496

THE PERSON WHO CHANGED MY LIFE

THE PERSON WHO CHANGED MY LIFE

Prominent Americans Recall Their Mentors

EDITED BY
Matilda Raffa Cuomo

FOREWORD BY
Hillary Rodham Clinton

A Birch Lane Press Book
Published by Carol Publishing Group

A Birch Lane Press Book
Published by Carol Publishing Group
Birch Lane Press is a registered trademark of Carol Communications, Inc.

Editorial, sales and distribution, rights and permissions inquiries should be addressed to Carol Publishing Group, 120 Enterprise Avenue, Secaucus, N.J. 07094

In Canada: Canadian Manda Group, One Atlantic Avenue, Suite 105, Toronto, Ontario M6K 3E7

Carol Publishing Group books may be purchased in bulk at special discounts for sales promotion, fund-raising, or educational purposes. Special editions can be created to specifications. For details, contact Special Sales Department, 120 Enterprise Avenue, Secaucus, N.J. 07094.

Manufactured in the United Sates of America
10 9 8 7 6 5 4 3 2 1

Library of Congress Cataloging-in-Publication Data
The person who changed my life : prominent Americans recall their mentors / edited by Matilda Cuomo ; foreword by Hillary Rodham Clinton.
p. cm.
ISBN 1-55972-508-7 (hardcover)
1. Self-actualization (Psychology) 2. Motivation (Psychology) 3. Mentoring. I. Cuomo, Matilda.
BF637.S4P445 1999
371.102—dc21 98-56541
CIP

To my husband, Mario,
our children and grandchildren.
May you always have faith, hope, and love.
May your light shine all the days of your lives.

CONTENTS

FOREWORD

I FIRST MET Matilda Raffa Cuomo when our husbands served as governors. I remember how much I immediately liked her and how passionately she talked about the importance of mentoring in the lives of our young people. She explained her efforts in New York to launch the nation's first statewide, one-to-one mentoring program. Over the years, at events at the White House or in New York, Matilda and I have continued our conversations about what mentoring has meant in our own lives, and our common commitment to open up those same opportunities to all children.

I am grateful to so many people—teachers, coaches, neighbors—who encouraged, supported, and challenged me while I was growing up. I will always be thankful to Rev. Donald James, my church's youth minister in Park Ridge, Illinois, who did so much to open a wider world to me and my friends. He arranged for our church youth group to worship and participate in service projects together with black and Hispanic teenagers in Chicago. He exposed us to modern art and poetry, from Picasso to e. e. cummings, long before school did. And in 1961 he took a group of us to hear Dr. Martin Luther King Jr. speak. As I listened to Dr. King's powerful words about nonviolence and the right of all Americans to live in dignity, I knew my world would never be the same.

Adults can have mentors, too. I had one after I met Marian Wright Edelman during my first year of Yale Law School. Marian, a civil rights lawyer and children's advocate, inspired my own commitment to justice. Marian also knows about mentoring. As she writes about growing up in South Carolina before the civil rights era, she describes how she and her sisters "were wrapped up and rocked in the cradle of faith, song, prayer, ritual, and worship, which immunized our spirits against some of the meanness and unfairness of our segregated South." I have felt that cloak of protection working in my own life. And I have seen how parents, church leaders, teachers, and other caring adults have sustained and supported young people in times of sorrow, pain, or confusion.

This book is filled with stories of people who were lucky enough to be embraced by that same loving web of relationships, and who, as a result, found the strength and direction to overcome barriers to success and freedom. Their stories underscore what we know by experience to be true—that even one caring adult in the life of a young person can make all the difference in the world, opening up opportunities that may have seemed unimaginable.

Every child needs a champion. Yet, for too many of America's children today, there are no champions; there are no mentors. Some young people may need tutoring help in school so they can feel the satisfaction of reading a good book and being promoted to the next class. Others may need coaching in a sport so they can experience what it is like to be engaged in team effort. Many children thrive when they are given the opportunity to contribute, whether in building a home for a homeless person or tutoring a young sibling or classmate. Every young person needs someone to say, "I believe in you."

I've seen the power of mentoring firsthand. For example, I have visited the Harriet Tubman School in Harlem, New York, where parents and members of the community were coming together to create after-school programs that are currently boosting students' grades and self-confidence. I have seen the excitement in the eyes of young inner-city children in Washington, D.C., as they looked forward to meeting with volunteers from Americorps who were helping them with their reading skills. And I have seen what can happen when artists, poets, and musicians unleash the creative imaginations of young people, turning a dreary classroom into a set for a play or a place to explore the wonders of a flute or a paintbrush.

Mentoring. Tutoring. After-school programs. There are many opportunities for caring, responsible adults to become involved in the lives of our children. At a time when there seems to be so little that people agree on, this is one mission worthy of bipartisan, broad-based support. It is not only the right thing to do, it is the smart thing to do. We know from countless studies that there are direct links between mentoring and tutoring programs and higher academic achievement, lower dropout rates, fewer teen pregnancies, and safer communities.

I hope this book will inspire more people to become involved in the life of a young person because we all have a critical role to play. I also hope it will persuade governors and legislators to invest more of their budgets in mentoring and other support programs for our young people. I am pleased that my husband recently signed into law the High Hopes Scholarship Fund, which will encourage middle schoolers in some of our poorest neighborhoods to begin thinking about going to college, and recruit mentors to help them make that dream a reality. The government clearly has a role to play. But, in the end, it is up to each and every one of us to become involved in a child's life.

There are many successful mentoring programs across the country that are making a difference in the lives of young people, thanks to leaders like Matilda Cuomo. Whether people enlist in a local mentoring program, informally start helping a child, or participate in national efforts like Mentoring USA, "I Have a Dream" programs, or the Boys and Girls Clubs of America, the result is the same. By giving one-to-one attention to a troubled child, offering hope where there is only despair, or opening doors that were once shut, we *can* change lives. These are some of the best investments we can make to ensure that children not only survive, but thrive in today's world.

For America to succeed in the twenty-first century everyone deserves a good education, and everyone should have the opportunity to go to college. We cannot afford to let only the privileged have those chances and dream those dreams. As a nation we must ensure that all children, regardless of their race, neighborhood, or family income, have the opportunity to fulfill their God-given potential and the skills they need to grow and flourish. Let us teach our children that they can go as far as their dreams and abilities will take them. Let us stand beside them, believe in them, and help guide them, until they get there.

Hillary Rodham Clinton

INTRODUCTION

ABOUT A YEAR AGO, I was brainstorming with my staff and family about creative outreach and strategies to promote mentoring. My daughter, Madeline, suggested a book project—a compilation of personal stories about influential mentors written by outstanding individuals from all walks of life, including the worlds of politics, entertainment, business, and the arts.

I thought this would be a perfect way to persuade potential volunteers that their efforts really do make a difference in the life of a child. The process proved to be an invaluable work experience—much more rewarding than I could ever have imagined.

My involvement with mentoring began in 1986, when my husband shared with me the alarming school dropout rate in New York State and the necessity of finding a good strategy to encourage children to stay in school. He asked for ideas about how to ameliorate this problem, and I told him that all my experiences as a child, a teacher, and a mother seemed to point to one solution: match every at-risk child with a caring, trained volunteer adult—a mentor. He agreed, and together we gathered a statewide committee of volunteers with expertise in all the relevant areas of child development. They were called upon to develop a plan of action, which they did with enthusiasm and efficiency. Mentoring was to be one of the state's major programs, reaching children at an early age before destructive habits became too complex to address. It was also decided that mentoring on a one-to-one basis would ensure the best results.

In 1987, the New York State Mentoring Program was established as the first statewide, school-based, one-to-one volunteer mentoring program in the country, serving children from kindergarten through eighth grade. At the time, mentoring was not as well known and understood as it is today, so our first mission was to introduce it to important community leaders around the state. After the first several months, hundreds of chief executive officers (CEOs), school administrators, teachers, politicians, and neighborhood activists were telling other potential volunteers about the adventures of Odysseus in the Trojan War and how he left his beloved son Telemachus in the care of "Mentor," his trusted counselor and loyal friend. Now the term *mentoring* is popular all over America.

The New York State Mentoring Program proved to be a successful model. It emphasizes a team approach that links parents, teachers, and mentors as essential partners in every child's success. If one of these aspects of a child's life is missing or dysfunctional, then the child is likely to perform poorly in school, make bad choices, and not achieve his or her full potential. The evidence is all around us. Too many children in America are struggling to find their way through the perils of drugs, alcohol, and dangerous permissiveness without good adult role models. They depend on school administrators or their teachers to designate a mentor. Without anyone to turn to for help, they would have very little hope for the future.

I was luckier than many of these children and, like many of our mentors, I wanted to share some of my own good fortune with today's troubled young people. Like many first-generation Americans growing up in the 1940s, I missed kindergarten and began school in the first grade, as required by law. At the time, there was little interaction between families and schools, and little tolerance for non–English-speaking immigrants, like my parents. I remember the pain of witnessing my mother's embarrassment when the principal brusquely ordered us to leave school because my mother was unable to fill out the enrollment forms for kindergarten. As we walked home she squeezed my hand, and I watched her eyes fill with tears of embarrassment and frustration. This memory has always reminded me of the resilience, courage, and love it took for her to raise five children. Mentors try to bring some of that strength to those they mentor.

When I attended P.S. 137 in Brooklyn, I was shy and insecure, unwilling to speak or assert myself in class. The first person to single me out for the encouragement I needed was Mrs. Kulyer, my fourth-grade teacher, who took the time to talk to me, draw me out, and share my thoughts about what I might do when I grew up. She was my first mentor beyond my parents. When Mrs. Kulyer told me I would make a great teacher, a whole world opened up. I rushed home to tell my parents the good news, and I never forgot her advice. Years later, I was teaching second grade in a public school in Elmont, Long Island.

My good fortune in being befriended by my fourth-grade teacher and other mentoring figures taught me that the reassurance of a devoted parent might not be enough for a child, especially one passing through the turbulence of preadolescence. Reflecting on my own years as a parent of five children, it is clear to me now that if I had been a single parent struggling to raise a family and earn a living, the need for outside support would have been essential. And the school would have been a good place to find that support.

For that reason, the New York State Mentoring Program looked for and found strong allies in school principals and teachers. The instant success of the program was proof that placing children first has an impact on all aspects of family and community life. We learned that children, matched with responsible volunteer mentors, demonstrated more confidence and a greater interest in school, increasing their chances of finishing high school and moving on to higher education or productive, fulfilling jobs. Between 1987 and 1995, we served ten thousand children from Buffalo to Long Island through the prodigious efforts of thousands of volunteers from all walks of life—corporations, government, and the community.

In 1995, after my husband left public service, the New York State Mentoring Program was discontinued by the new state administration. I was saddened by the development, but with my family's encouragement, I established Mentoring USA as a private, nonprofit organization.

My son, Andrew, is now secretary of the Department of Housing and Urban Development. In 1987 he founded HELP USA, which has been managed and expanded under the leadership of my daughter, Maria Cuomo Cole, who is currently its chairperson. HELP USA has become the nation's largest builder, developer, and operator of transitional housing, with comprehensive, on-site human services for the homeless. It was clear from experience that the children in the HELP USA facilities would benefit from the caring relationship that Mentoring USA could provide.

Mentoring USA continues the model and mission of the original New York State Mentoring Program and has expanded to become national, and even international. We've learned that both the problems children face and the efficacy of mentoring in solving these problems are truly universal. Indeed, I am often reminded of one of my father's favorite expressions, *"Tutto il mondo é paese"*—"all the world is one."

Today, Mentoring USA functions as a school-based and community site-based mentoring program. The mentors partner with the community, the schools, the government, and the private sector to form a unified team to help the children. Our volunteer mentors, who are carefully screened and trained, make a commitment to work with their children on a one-to-one basis for a minimum of four hours a month for one year. These efforts have helped motivate and encourage thousands of children to stay in school, avoid drugs and teenage pregnancy, and gain self-confidence and hope for the future. Every child who benefits is a small miracle.

When I was first lady of New York, I mentored two girls in the Albany area. I met Ely, a shy, withdrawn girl with limited English proficiency, when she was in the fourth grade. I was assigned to mentor Ely because I could understand and speak a little Spanish. She was good at math, but had trouble with other subjects, especially English and social studies. For Ely, having another strong adult influence was crucial; her mother was a single parent, was not well educated, and faced all the difficulties of raising her four children alone. At first, Ely found it hard to believe that someone outside her family wanted to help her. She looked at me one day and asked, "Why are you taking time for me? You don't even like me!" She was echoing the sentiments of thousands of children throughout the country living in difficult circumstances with little self-esteem and a tragically premature cynicism about life.

During our four years together, Ely grew and matured, and our relationship flourished. She became more expressive and confident, and went on to finish Albany High School. This year she will graduate from Hudson Community College, and intends to use her accounting skills to work in a bank and continue her education. She understands the difference a mentor made in her life, and is now the role model for her three younger siblings.

Like Ely, Brittany, the second child I mentored, also came from a single-parent household and needed extra support. She was not applying herself at school and had to improve her work habits as well as her social skills. The one-to-one relationship she had with me gave her a different perspective on life. Not only did Brittany benefit from our relationship, but her mother, perhaps for the first time, realized that she was not alone. Brittany's mother, like Brittany herself, grew in self-confidence. She was able to develop her skills to find a part-time job and is now working full-time. Both Brittany and Ely proved to me that one-to-one mentoring is an early intervention strategy that can help a child do well in school and beyond, with long-lasting benefits to the family and community.

Everyone in Mentoring USA derives satisfaction from its successes and their involvement in our program. We are painfully aware of how many children are still waiting for a mentor. In New York City, Mayor Rudolph Giuliani proposed that we help children living in New York City Housing Authority sites, and Schools' Chancellor Rudolph Crew challenged Mentoring USA to help students perform to expected standards in his designated Chancellor's District schools.

During the past three years, many corporations and foundations have generously supported our efforts. Our major corporate partners—Conair Corporation, Prudential Insurance Company, Merrill Lynch, Andersen Consulting, Van Cleef and Arpels, AT&T, Bell Atlantic, Con Edison, Federated Department Stores, and Fleet Bank—have donated funds and services, and have encouraged their staff to volunteer to be mentors. Countless individuals have also contributed to and assisted in the expansion of Mentoring USA.

Community organizations and universities across the country that have partnered with Mentoring USA include the National Italian American Foundation, Women's American ORT, the Junior League of New York, the Young Men's Christian Association (YMCA) of Greater New York, Sigma Gamma Rho Sorority, the Democratic Women's Leadership Forum, New York Cares, New York University's C-Team, St. John's University, San Diego State University, Fordham University, Mt. St. Vincent's College, Mercy College, and Harvard University.

Many government agencies have also supported the Mentoring USA model, the New York City Council under the leadership of Speaker Peter Vallone, including the Brooklyn District Attorney's office, the California Conservation Corps, the U.S. Internal Revenue Service, the New York State Department of Education, the New York City Sanitation Department, the Metropolitan Transit Authority, the California Department of Transportation, and the San Diego Police, Health, and Fire departments.

Over the years, however, our largest single source of mentors has been the New York City Police Department (NYPD). First working with Commissioner William Bratton and now with the cooperation of current commissioner, Howard Safir, New York's finest has proven once again that they are dedicated to community service. Since 1997, over six hundred NYPD uniformed and civilian staff have volunteered to be mentors, and they are the linchpins of some of our programs.

Many children who "graduate" from the Mentoring USA program in eighth grade still need a mentoring relationship in high school. We are in the process of establishing relationships with high school mentoring programs whose goals include job shadowing, college preparation, instruction in the practicalities of job searches, and providing all the support needed to help children prepare for the future.

Over the years, Mentoring USA has encouraged children to learn about their own culture as well as the cultures and traditions of others. BRAVE resource collections (an acronym for Bias-Related

Anti-Violence Education) has been developed in select schools and community centers where we have our mentoring programs. The collections includes books, videotapes, and other materials on the lives of heroic individuals who have fought prejudice, violence, racial bias, and intolerance. BRAVE supports the efforts of our mentors to instill, in the children they mentor, self-esteem, respect for cultural diversity, and pride in one's heritage.

For more than a decade, we have encouraged public officials to keep children high on the list of government priorities. In recent years, more and more of them have responded favorably. At this time there are some governors who have made mentoring children a priority. The National Mentoring Partnership is taking the lead to encourage statewide mentoring initiatives.

In April 1997, President Bill Clinton convened the Presidents' Summit on America's Future in Philadelphia, where mentoring was highlighted as an effective strategy for helping at-risk children. I was invited to make a presentation about Mentoring USA and its mission. The summit reinforced what we knew from over ten years of experience—that providing a caring adult mentor on a one-to-one basis can help a child academically and emotionally. And Hillary Rodham Clinton continues the momentum with her recent mentoring initiative at the White House.

In recent reports, many authorities, including Public/Private Ventures and the Commonwealth Fund, have arrived at essentially the same conclusions—that children who are matched with mentors demonstrate a greater interest in school, increased discipline in performing tasks, and a more positive attitude, which lowers their chances of becoming drug users, teenage parents, or high school dropouts. Hopefully, the federal government and the state's leaders will take their cue from these studies and will make substantial commitments to after-school programs—especially those that offer mentoring.

For programs like Mentoring USA and Mentoring USA/Italia, the work of fund-raising can be difficult, occasionally discouraging, and always time consuming. However, the growing number of success stories of mentors and the mentored is all the encouragement we need to continue. David Porter, a New York police officer, has spoken about his own satisfaction at being able to reach a child early rather than later, when the only contact a young person may have with the police may be crime related. Another mentor, Sion Batesh, a young, self-employed entrepreneur, talked about the joy of being able to broaden another's perspective, speaking as the child he mentored stood by his side at a recent mentoring conference at St. John's University.

More wonderful proof of the effectiveness of mentoring comes from those men and women whose stories we have included in the book, individuals who have risen to the top of their fields, distinguishing themselves in great and small ways. Walter Cronkite once said that no one does anything in life on his own, that there are always caring people who shape our lives and our careers, whose influence stays with us for the rest of our lives. These essays are a testimony to this truth, and a tribute to all the people who have helped shape the lives of children.

It is clear that the mentors who have been brought to life in these essays have not been forgotten, and they are, in every sense of the word, true heroes and heroines. It is my fervent hope that the stories of these admired and successful men and women will inspire many others to make similar investments in the future of children. Mentoring is a lifetime investment for a child; children will always remember their mentors with joy and gratitude, and mentors themselves will also have a fulfilling memory to cherish.

Matilda Raffa Cuomo

ACKNOWLEDGMENTS

THIS EXTRAORDINARY UNDERTAKING has brought together many wonderful people and it is my privilege to thank all of them. This book had its conception in the bright mind and great sensitivity of a young lawyer, mother, and mentored-turned-mentor—my daughter, Madeline Cuomo O'Donoghue. Madeline thought up the idea, urged me to do it, and helped get it done. Thank you, Madeline!

When I mentioned Madeline's book idea to Walter Cronkite he was instantly supportive, saying that no one does everything by themselves in life and that we should always remember the people who help us.

My deepest gratitude goes to our nation's First Lady, Hillary Rodham Clinton, who, despite the enormous demands made upon her, found the time to contribute an eloquent and thoughtful foreword expressing the importance of mentoring for children. She has always been a special source of inspiration and encouragement to us at Mentoring USA.

Thanks to Leonard Riggio, president of Barnes and Noble, Jim Griffin and Mel Berger of the William Morris Agency, and Andrew Miller, who gave me direction and guidance. With patience and commitment, Mel Berger procured Carol Publishing Group and the sage counsel of Hillel Black.

I must also thank Carolyn Hanson for her initial input. She laid the foundation and structure, which gave us a very good start. Her outstanding effort was built upon by Stuart McDaniel, and I thank him for conducting the interviews enthusiastically and professionally. Special gratitude to my dear friend Billy Baldwin for all his encouragement and assistance with his family's participation. Charles Lyons, president of the U.S. Committee for UNICEF, believed in this project early on and offered his assistance, promoting the work nationally and internationally through the UNICEF catalogue.

This book would not have been possible without the truly relentless efforts of two stalwarts at Mentoring USA: Stephen Menchini, its director, who helped organize this extraordinary project and shepherd it to conclusion, and Junnko Tozaki, through the understanding and expertise she brought to this venture.

My thanks, also, to the members of our Mentoring USA family, to managing directors Maggie Shaw and Charmaine Crawford, and Special Assistant Anne Taibleson, for their devoted service, especially in the moments of special need.

A warm embrace for Ely and Brittany, whom I mentored, and who inspired me to expand the mentoring program. Through their own personal growth, they have demonstrated so vividly the extraordinary usefulness of mentoring.

Every member of my family fortifies me in their own unique ways, especially my husband, Mario. They are the precious jewels of my life and helped make this worthwhile effort a joy. With tremendous appreciation, we thank all the participants for their generosity, compassion, and special devotion to children. They have made all of our lives better.

THE PERSON WHO CHANGED MY LIFE

DANA GLUCKSTEIN

EDWARD ASNER

Versatile, committed, eloquent, and talented are all adjectives that describe actor and activist Edward Asner. Perhaps best known for his award-winning comic and dramatic portrayal of journalist Lou Grant, Asner achieved a crossover with this character that most actors only dream about.

He has been the recipient of seven Emmy and five Golden Globe Awards, and served as national president of the Screen Actors Guild for two terms. He was inducted into the TV Academy Hall of Fame in 1996. Active in many humanitarian and political organizations, his boundless energy is divided between his dramatic projects and political and charitable causes.

Mr. Asner has recently completed three films waiting distribution, titled *Fanatics, Prep,* and *Perfect Game.*

TWO MEN WHO SERVED in World War II before returning to careers in the Kansas City public schools were my mentors: my high school football coach, Ed Ellis, and my journalism teacher, George Corporon.

Corporon, who had served as a battlefield historian, came back looking frail, as if he had been witness to a great many things. He never burdened us with them, but instilled in us an awe and respect for journalism as it should be. I was the first guy he let edit the paper while playing football. He was probably the most intellectual of my then-teachers, which intrigued me, and he stimulated me to know more of the world and the finer things in it.

One of the most significant exchanges I had with Coach Ellis happened before I actually played for him. I would see him around my best friend's house fairly often, because he and my friend's father, the swim coach, were great pals. He was a charming and wonderful man with a great spirit and the ability to fill those around him with it. This particular afternoon I was ranting and raving about the striking coal miners, having been led to believe by the Republican newspapers that punitive measures should be taken. Coach Ellis simply and totally rebuked me: "Well, Ed. You can't take away a man's right to strike."

I was so shocked by his answer, which flew in the face of prevailing opinion in my hometown, that it kept me in awe of him forever after and helped me to become a union man.

Both George Corporon and Coach Ellis showed me what quality and higher stature should look like and what I should aspire to. They helped inculcate in me a deep sense of fairness, by their words and the even more impressive example of their own behavior, which continues to inform every sphere of my life, from the political to the personal to the professional. I grew up in Kansas City as the youngest of a large clan. To have adults in my life who didn't see me as the baby of the family but as an individual—a knowledgeable and capable individual—was very good for me.

The major turning points in my life—discovering a passion for acting in my first college production, landing the part of Lou

Grant, being elected president of the Screen Actor's Guild, among others—didn't, of course, happen out of the blue. They were each just one of many possible consequences of a whole string of earlier events, decisions, and happy accidents.

So, no, Coach Ellis never suggested I give up football for the school play. But he and George Corporon and all the other good people I was lucky enough to have in my early life did help make me into someone with the self-knowledge and self-confidence to pursue the things that really mattered to me. They gave me the solid foundation that made everything possible. They had a real impact, not just on my life, but on the lives of so many young people. And all with very little noise. Their influence make me realize that there's too much glory when I do something (or sometimes opprobrium, but mostly glory).

It's people like them, whose contributions aren't written up in the press or recognized with awards and applause, who really knock my socks off: the people who struggle as labor organizers; nurses who go far beyond the call of duty; caring teachers who often spend their own money so their kids can go farther; social workers, who perform one of the roughest jobs in the world, a job that eats you up, but they constantly find ways to help the less fortunate; people who run soup kitchens and missions; and, above all, the anonymous donors of this world.

Alec Baldwin

GREG GORMAN

Alec Baldwin began his acting career in 1979 while attending undergraduate school of drama at New York University (NYU), studying at the Lee Strasberg Theatre Institute. In 1993 he returned to complete his undergraduate studies, receiving a B.F.A. degree in drama. Along with his brothers William, Stephen, and Daniel, all actors, he is helping to build the Baldwin family acting dynasty.

Debuting in 1986 in Joe Orton's black comedy *Loot*, Mr. Baldwin has appeared onstage in a variety of productions, including *Prelude to a Kiss, Macbeth, A Streetcar Named Desire*, and David Mamet's *A Life in the Theater.*

Mr. Baldwin has acted in numerous films, such as *Beetlejuice, Married to the Mob, Glengarry Glen Ross, The Shadow, Ghosts of Mississippi*, and *The Edge.* He recently completed *The Confession*, the first film produced by his own production company, El Dorado Pictures.

Alec is the president of the Creative Coalition, and a

benefactor of the Bay Street Theatre Festival in Sag Harbor, New York, People for the American Way, the City Center of New York, and the Drama League of New York. He is also a supporter of the Hudson Riverkeeper and People for the Ethical Treatment of Animals.

He is married to actress Kim Basinger, with whom he has a daughter, Ireland Eliesse.

ELAINE AIKEN WAS MY ACTING COACH and friend for nearly twenty years before she died of cancer in 1998. I first met Elaine at the Lee Strasberg Theatre Institute, where she taught acting classes. Although not a student of hers back in 1979, I began studying with her privately a few years after I left school. Elaine was an intelligent, fiercely opinionated, loving, and confident woman, someone who took acting quite seriously, but not so much as to be paralyzed by its inherent self-consciousness and self-delusions.

Acting is an art form that, above all, requires courage, and Elaine Aiken instilled in her students the valuable lesson that renewal of that courage is essential for creativity to thrive. She asked her students to consider their limitations, or at least their perceived limitations, and to wonder if they might overcome them with simple and focused effort.

When I performed in *A Streetcar Named Desire* on Broadway, there was a detached sexuality and languid masculinity in the character of Stanley Kowalski that we both agreed was a direction I should go. Now, I don't know how sexually cool and languidly masculine I appeared, but Elaine's work with me on that character, on the simple truth that Stanley had doubts about who he was and what he wanted in this world, led me to one of the most pleasurable experiences of my career.

Elaine Aiken gave me the greatest gifts one can give to a friend: love and support. And she gave me the greatest gifts that a teacher can give to a student: confidence and passion. Without my friendship with Elaine, I do not believe that I would have enjoyed my work as much as I have these past twenty years.

CAROL BALDWIN

FERNANDO

Breast-cancer survivor Carol Martineau Baldwin has dedicated her life to finding a cure for breast cancer. A Syracuse native and a graduate of Syracuse University, she and her husband, Alexander, raised their family in Massapequa, Long Island. In 1983, after twenty-nine years of marriage, her husband died of lung cancer, and in 1990, Carol was diagnosed with breast cancer.

Although she had moved back to Syracuse after her family was grown, Carol always maintained strong ties to Long Island and, in 1996, with a sharp awareness of the very high breast-cancer rate in the region, formed the Carol M. Baldwin Breast-Cancer Research Fund, Inc. The sole purpose of the corporation is to raise money for breast-cancer research at University Hospital and Medical Center at Stony Brook, one of the nation's top three public research institutions.

Carol is the mother of actors Alec, Daniel, Stephen, and William Baldwin.

WHEN I WAS GROWING UP we had a housekeeper, "Auntie" May. My mom was ill and many of the maternal responsibilities in the house fell to this wonderful woman. She was an amazing person who managed to keep our brood of six girls and one boy in a nonchaotic state for over twenty-five years. My family and extended family taught us to be understanding, not angry, and to channel anger into something productive. Perhaps that is why I am so actively involved in the crusade to cure breast cancer today.

As a young bride I left home to live with my husband in Massapequa, Long Island. This was my first real time away from home, and I had to draw on some of the domestic family experiences that Auntie May had shared with me. As a young girl, I couldn't go out unless my room was neat and my chores finished. She taught us how to bake and how to use the washing machine. Today I love to bake, but I am not so sure about washing clothes. May helped me create a home for my new family, and carry into adulthood some of the life lessons that were part of my childhood.

My father Roy was also an important influence in my life. When my own family began to grow I often thought of him and his very basic values. When I was a child we would visit Lake Ontario, and he would find endless pleasure in the simple things of life, including skipping rocks across the lake. He told me what I have hopefully passed on to my own children: never let a child think they can't do something. They must try, for success will come when the child finds the correct niche. If they fail, they will still know they have tried. From that lesson they will learn something and ultimately go on to success.

I am not an activist but a member of the crusade, made stronger by many thousands of volunteers who share my commitment to eradicate breast cancer. I am proud and grateful to all who helped me reach this point in my life.

DANIEL BALDWIN

NEIL JACOBS

After starring in the highly acclaimed television series *Homicide: Life on the Street,* Daniel Baldwin made a commitment to diversify his talents in film and television. He has since appeared on film in Steve Buscemi's *Trees Lounge* and Lee Tamahori's *Mulholland Falls* with Nick Nolte, Melanie Griffith, and John Malkovich. Baldwin will soon be seen starring in *The Treat,* written and directed by *Mars Attacks* scree writer Jonathan Gems, and *Phoenix* with Ray Liotta. Along with brothers Alec, William, and Stephen, he is helping to build the Baldwin family acting dynasty.

It was Baldwin's role as Beau Felton, the detective preoccupied with his troubled marriage, in the NBC Emmy-winning series *Homicide: Life on the Street,* which earned the actor wide-audience popularity. Baldwin has appeared in a wide variety of motion pictures, from Oliver Stone's *Born on the Fourth of July* to Dan Aykroyd's *Nothing But Trouble.*

The actor continues a variety of athletic activities, many of which he played in college, including football, basketball, baseball, golf, wrestling, and boxing.

MICHAEL AND ELIZABETH WELT were the parents of seven children and neighbors of ours on Long Island. I was very close to two of their children: Michael, who was a year older and quarterback of the football team; and Mary Anne, who was in my grade and a good friend. But I was close to the parents as well.

Mr. Welt was a very calm and patient man, very self-assured. There was something special about him—some sort of special presence—that seemed to result from the combination of his voice and vocal delivery. He had a real storyteller's voice. He was also a very wise man, ready to give advice on many issues. He helped me a lot in this respect. I felt that I could talk to him about anything.

Five years ago I suddenly thought of him and decided to call. It had been some time since I had talked with any of the Welts. We spoke of all the kids, but when I asked about Mrs. Welt there was a pause. He told me that she had passed away. I started stammering my apologies and condolences, horrified that I hadn't heard of her death. He replied very calmly that maybe I should call more often.

I was so upset that I couldn't sleep for several nights. Finally I flew to New York, took the train to Long Island and went straight to the Welt house. When Mr. Welt opened the door I told him how upset I was at the news of Mrs. Welt's passing, and kept repeating my apologies. We sat on the stoop and talked for awhile, but when I broke down we moved into the kitchen. Sitting in the room that had served as a second home for me brought back so many memories.

It's difficult for me to go back to Long Island since my family moved away. There just doesn't seem to be that much there for me anymore. When I see people I grew up with it is sometimes awkward. It is difficult to return to a place when you've stepped outside of that world. But, in a good way, a lot hasn't changed. The beauty that's there will never go away.

When I called Mr. Welt to ask his permission to call him my mentor for this book he of course wanted to know in what context I was going to discuss him. That's his way of joking—very dry. When he asked how I was doing, I started talking about everything I was involved in, but he stopped me and said, "No, Daniel, how are *you* doing?" I had to pause and laugh. He always cuts right through everything and gets down to business. "I'm doing fine," I told him. "I'm doing fine."

"Life is an adventure," he told me. "Get behind the wheel and just go. Don't look back. Just go."

The Welts will always hold a special place in my heart. They were that other family in the neighborhood with a lot of kids who always had a meal at their house for me. And they always had time for me, whether to laugh, give advice, or just talk. I never met a finer woman than Mrs. Welt, and Mr. Welt has always been a rock of consistency for me, a good friend. They have meant so much to me.

ANDREW ECCLES

STEPHEN BALDWIN

Not being exempt from the Baldwin family gene pool, Stephen, the youngest of four brothers, all actors, enrolled in the American Academy of Dramatic Arts in his late teens, marking the start of his acting career. Along with his brothers Daniel, Alec, and William he is helping to build the Baldwin family acting dynasty.

After an array of guest-starring roles, Stephen went on to star in the ABC series *The Young Riders,* portraying the legendary William "Buffalo Bill" Cody. His film credits include *One Tough Cop, Friends and Lovers, The Usual Suspects, Threesome,* and his debut film, *Born on the Fourth of July.*

Stephen devotes a great deal of his spare time to philanthropic endeavors. He was the creator, organizer, and host of Pool Aid, a celebrity pool tournament (1993–96) and Fore Play, a celebrity golf tournament. This year he is creating and hosting the First Annual Carol M. Baldwin Celebrity Golf Tournament to benefit his mother's foundation—the Carol M. Baldwin Breast Cancer Research Fund, Inc.

In his spare time, Stephen reads and writes poetry, indulges his passion for music, and loves spending time with his wife and two daughters.

DR. JAMES FEARING is known throughout the world as the Crisis Doctor because of his work as a drug and alcohol rehabilitative interventionist. He also works in other fields, such as motivational work for businesses, athletic leagues and teams, and celebrities. He helps children with computer addiction. In his successful program Executive Time Out, Dr. Fearing takes business executives on anti-stress retreats, where he seeks to provide them with positive ways to deal with the stress of their daily living and the issues that stress might cause. He seeks to implement these positive changes as an aspect of their lives after they return from the retreat.

I met Dr. Fearing when he was helping an actor in Hollywood with substance abuse problems. Sobriety drew us together, and in my ten years in the entertainment industry I have referred him to many people and seen the results of his work with them.

Alcoholism and drug addiction is a depressing situation. The addicted individual doesn't know which direction to go and feels that there's no way out of the dark place that they are in. Dependence on any substance is a horrible feeling, the powerlessness that an addicted person experiences cannot be measured or fully expressed. Dr. Fearing has a format that helps to guide an individual out of this dark place where they find themselves.

The things that I have learned since becoming sober have been fascinating. My life has become so much richer. It's empowered me to become an example for others in the Hollywood community. People can't believe it when they find out that I don't drink; they perceive me as some wild crazy party guy. But I didn't enjoy where alcohol took me.

I don't feel that I have to specify or qualify my experience of substance abuse to other—it's really no one's business—and I'm not a spokesman for sobriety. But if someone wants to discuss it because they feel that they may need help, then I'll be specific about my experience. This usually happens about once a year, when I sit and talk to someone for awhile about my own experience and what I found worked for me. And then I usually refer them to Dr. Fearing.

Dr. Fearing once explained his view of alcoholism to me; it is a tricky disease. When you get cancer, or AIDS, there are symptoms. But alcoholism is the only disease that tells the person suffering from it that nothing is wrong. It tells you to drink more and you don't know it.

Dr. Fearing lives, eats, sleeps, and breathes changing people's lives. He opens their eyes to life and helps them realize the precious gift of living. It is amazing to watch and experience the process of his work. He gives people the freedom to claim a new lease on life. But he doesn't fix people—he teaches them ways to fix themselves.

William Baldwin

HERB RITTS

William Baldwin launched his film career with a role in Oliver Stone's *Born on the Fourth of July.* His recent starring roles include the Raul Ruiz film *Shattered Image,* with Anne Parillaud; Universal's *Virus,* with Jamie Lee Curtis and Donald Sutherland; and Miramax's *Curdled.*

Despite the demands of an acting career, Baldwin has maintained his social and political activism. He is the newly elected president of the Creative Coalition, an organization dedicated to raising awareness in the arts and entertainment community on issues ranging from health care to environmental concerns and federal arts funding. He is also a member of the board of HELP USA, which is dedicated to solving the problems of housing for the homeless, and of Rock the Vote, which promotes voter participation and raises awareness about censorship. He presently lives in New York with his wife Chynna Phillips. Along with his brothers Stephen, Daniel, and Alec, he is also helping to build the Baldwin family acting dynasty.

MY FATHER ALEC WAS THE GREATEST mentor, role model, and inspiration in my life, and he also influenced the lives of many other young people. He was a teacher and coach at Massapequa High School on Long Island for thirty-two years, and he got involved in many extracurricular programs. Indeed, my father was a pillar of our community. There were not many individuals or families whose lives were not touched by or who had not benefited from my father's kindness, generosity, devotion, wisdom, and spirit. I was extremely lucky during my childhood, because, while my father did not enjoy the luxury of material comforts or wealth, there was no shortage of love, support, stability, and guidance.

Aside from my own parents, Al and Cathy Bevilacqua were, without question, the greatest influences in my life. Their home was down the block and around the corner from ours. I vividly remember sitting at their kitchen table during many late, hot summer evenings talking with Mrs. Bevilacqua. We would have many philosophical and inspirational discussions about topics ranging from family to marriage to spirituality to education. She was a tremendous influence and inspiration to me during childhood. She was kind, generous, wise, spiritual, sensitive, and caring. She taught me to stimulate and challenge myself both intellectually and culturally. She also helped me to grow and evolve as a human being. She taught me to stay motivated, to be productive, to be of service, and to persevere. She continuously communicated these themes to me throughout my life, and still does today.

Her husband Al is a legendary figure in the sport of wrestling. He is one of the most influential, successful, respected, and celebrated coaches in the history of the sport. Coaching for him was never only about winning. It was about competition, discipline, commitment,work ethic, mental toughness, learning, and having fun, too. It was about instilling values and providing tools for young people to take with them for the rest of their lives. These tools would help produce productive, responsible, and respectable young adults, and they influence the way I think about life today. They are at the core of my existence, and I have the sport of wrestling and, more specifically, Al Bevilacqua to thank for it. For this, I am forever indebted to him.

Hopefully, everyone has the one schoolteacher from their childhood whom they remember, one who made an indelible impression, who inspired them and made a difference.

ANDREW ECCLES/ABC

JOY BEHAR

Joy Behar is among today's leading comic talents. She is seen daily as cohost on ABC television's hit program, *The View.* Whether mixing with the audience or interviewing politicians and artists, she dives into absurd juxtapositions, her aim being not to sneer but to reveal absurdities, especially those perpetrated by big guys on little ones. With a voice that sounds, as she says, "like I have Jimmy Hoffa in the back of my throat," she strips the varnish off pretensions.

Behar has appeared in such movies as *Cookie* with Peter Falk, *Love Is All There Is,* Nora Ephran's *This Is My Life,* and Woody Allen's *Manhattan Murder Mystery.* She recently completed a successful run of the off-Broadway hit *The Food Chain,* where she earned rave reviews in the starring role. Her last Broadway appearance was in Alexander H. Cohen's production of *Comedy Tonight,* with Mort Sahl and Dorothy London.

I HAD NO REAL DESIRE to try and be a professional actor or comedian. I was too shy and too scared. So I continued with my education, eventually got my master's degree in teaching and became a teacher. I taught all through my twenties, but inside I wanted to do something different. I really wanted to act; I wanted to try comedy. Finally, in my early thirties, I told myself that I would do it, and I did.

My Aunt Sadie always encouraged me to take risks. There were times when my mom would ask how much longer I was going to "try this comedy thing." In the routine I would say, "One more year,' and my mom would reply, "Six more months.'

Luckily for me, Aunt Sadie would intervene on my behalf. "You take as long as you need to," she would say. And I did. I took her intervention as a sign of her faith in me; she really believed in me and what I was striving for. My mother believed in me too, but she was more nervous about it.

Others who gave me support were female therapists. Luckily for me, I have had three amazing female therapists. Some people are embarrassed to admit that they're in therapy. Not me! These women really had a profound influence on my life. They helped me through some difficult times. I know of people who were in the arts whose therapists suggested they try another profession, not because they were maliciously trying to wreck their dreams, but because they believed it was the best course of action for them. However, my therapists were supportive of my pursuits and extremely encouraging. That made a great difference for me.

Another great role model for me is Barbara Walters. She is an extremely hard worker, doesn't complain, and does it all herself. And she never lets barriers stop or slow her down. She is at the top of her game, but even with her stature as a journalist, she still faces ageism and sexism. She has had to face many obstacles in the course of her career but nothing seems to bother her. It's amazing. She's amazing. Through her, you can see what it takes to be a successful woman.

MARC RABOY

HARRY BELAFONTE

Harry Belafonte has been called "the consummate entertainer"—an artist in every field in which he has participated—a concert singer, a recording artist, and a movie, Broadway, and television star and producer. His activity in the human rights struggle is universally lauded. His awards and recognitions encompass both worlds, as artist and humanitarian. He believes that his work for human rights and his artistic pursuits give him the basis for a most productive and balanced life. Neither overshadows the other, and both are extremely important to him.

Belafonte has dedicated his life to uniting people and doing battle for causes often considered controversial. He has been a cultural adviser to the Peace Corps, a member of the board of directors of the Southern Christian Leadership Conference, and the chairperson for the New York State

Martin Luther King Jr. Commission, to name a few of his roles as a leader. He is the recipient of numerous degrees and awards.

HAVING COME FROM an extremely dysfunctional family, as a young man I found myself in search of guidance. The guidance offered to me was rather meager. My mother, Millie, was a single parent. Although she was still married to my father, he was absent. In raising us, she did the best she could.

She told us that life was guided by values and wisdom. However, there were areas about growing up where she could not offer very much instruction. The little she did give was very meaningful to me.

So I searched for guidance. I walked through life seeking wisdom and truth but many of the places I went I found barren and devoid of meaning. These were difficult times for me. So much seemed out of reach.

I volunteered for the navy when I was seventeen, served two years, and at nineteen found myself back on the streets of New York searching for something to become. Quite by accident, I stumbled into the theater.

I first saw *Home Is a Hunter* at Harlem's American Negro Theater in 1946. It was directed by the artistic director and cofounder of the theater, Abram Hill. It was a profoundly moving experience. Here was a Black play, written by a Harlem playwright. It changed my life. I saw purpose, passion, and the impact the play had on the other theatergoers. I knew that I needed to get involved with this theater group.

The American Negro Theater, located at the 135th Street Library with a capacity of 125 people, was founded in 1940 by Abram Hill and Frederick O'Neal with the goal of eliminating the barriers of Black participation in the theater and portraying a more realistic and honest view of Black life. In addition to staging productions, the theater also served as a drama school and broadcast a weekly radio program. Community-oriented, the American Negro Theater was an amazing place to be as a young Black man in the 1940s.

The first play in which I performed there was *On Striver's Row,* a satire on social climbing. It was written and directed by Abram Hill, and proved a huge success for the theater. The next play in which I acted was Sean O'Casey's *Juno and the Paycock,* an Irish play Hill had reworked to reflect the Black American experience. It was brilliantly constructed and very successful. But it was the content of the play that appealed to me. I felt it was an act of social activism to perform it. The original illustrated the plight of the Irish against injustice and the difficulties they faced in their day-to-day lives. Reworked by Hill, it said a great deal about Black life in America.

Paul Robeson saw the show in our first week of performance. Afterward he talked with the cast and offered his support and criticism. Meeting the man changed my life. Robeson, the son of a runaway slave and an abolitionist, was a brilliant athlete, scholar, a valedictorian at Rutgers University, and a law graduate from Columbia University. He took a job in a law firm but quit the legal profession after a white secretary refused to take dictation from him. He turned his intellect and passion to the arts and social activism. He was a humanist, committed to the principles of the Constitution, and a quintessential Renaissance man. He spoke and sang fluently in fourteen languages!

I saw embodied in Paul Robeson everything I wanted to measure my life against. His political and social courage challenged me to better myself in all aspects of my life. As time went on, we became very good friends. It was from Paul that I learned that the purpose of art is not just to show life as it is, but to show life as it should be, and that if art were put into the service of the human family, it could only enhance it.

He was blacklisted by the House Un-American Activities Committee, which confiscated his passport, citing that he was a Communist. He fought the committee's action and eventually triumphed. His victory was a milestone for many Americans.

I was extremely blessed by his presence in my life. Had it not been for Paul, my life would have been much different. He continually inspired me to do more, to always push myself, and to help as many people I could in the continual struggle against injustice, not only in America, but worldwide. He was a true citizen of the world who cared nothing for political boundaries, but always strove to help people everywhere.

Toward the end of his life I asked him if all his struggles had been worth it. He said to me, "Harry, make no mistake, there is no aspect of what I have done that wasn't worth it. Although we may not have achieved all the goals we set for ourselves, and although some victories may have eluded us, the most important aspect was the journey itself and the people I met along the way and the friendships shared."

The one-hundred-year anniversary of his birth was marked in 1998. The celebration that took place at Carnegie Hall was filled with others, like myself, whose lives were changed and inspired by this amazing, remarkable, and special man.

Carol Bellamy

Carol Bellamy assumed office as the fourth director of the United Nation's Children's Fund (UNICEF), with the rank of undersecretary general of the United Nations, on May 1, 1995. Ms. Bellamy joined UNICEF from a position as director of the U.S. Peace Corps, a service organization. She was the first returned volunteer to serve as head of the Peace Corps, which has 6,500 volunteers in more than ninety countries.

Ms. Bellamy has worked extensively in the public sector, including five years in the New York State Senate (1973–77). In 1978, she became the first woman president of the New York Council, a position she held until 1985. Carol Bellamy is a graduate of Gettysburg College and holds a law degree from New York University. She is a former fellow of the Institute of Politics of the Kennedy School of Government at Harvard University.

Karen Burstein has been a friend and colleague since we met in the New York State Senate. She is a brilliant woman who influenced me because she pushed me to be more curious, to ask more questions, and to strive harder in all aspects of my life.

She has always impressed people, including myself, with her words in speeches and debates. Although her nature can be challenging at times—she can be very direct in her opinions and views—she is genuine in dealing with people. This is part of what makes her who she is, it is not a front with her.

In the New York State Senate in the 1970s, she was the impetus for a small group of women politicians to become more active, both politically and personally. I was a member of that group, and her friendship has been a delight to me.

Another influential period in my life resulted from my involvement in the Peace Corps, from 1963 to 1965, when I lived in Guatemala as a volunteer community developer. My job consisted of basic health work, such as immunizations and cultivating school gardens for nutrition. There were other parts to the job, but mainly simple things. This experience changed my outlook in many ways. My horizons expanded, and I gained significant insight and appreciation of a foreign country and culture.

My Peace Corps involvement also changed my direction in life. I was a kid fresh out of school and not particularly qualified for any "real" job. It was an experience that would later spill over into my business life, my legislative life—everything.

Volunteerism *can* be very powerful because it adds value to life for those you are helping and for yourself; it is a two-way street. Those being helped benefit just as much as the volunteer. It is a life-affirming experience.

You do not succeed in everything; you never will. But failure should never stop you from attempting to succeed. Self-knowledge, resulting from either success or failure, has many rewards whether you win or lose. It is in the struggle that we gain insight about ourselves, for we will know how much further, or how much harder, we must go the next time. The beauty of living exists in striving.

MARK SELIGER © 1998 SONY MUSIC

TONY BENNETT

Bennett's fifth decade in popular music has been perhaps his most rewarding, with the recognition his music has received from a new generation of listeners. According to the *New York Times*, Tony Bennett "has not just bridged the generation gap, he has demolished it. He has solidly connected with a younger crowd weaned on rock. And there have been no compromises." Perhaps one of the reasons why he's had a lasting success and impact is because he communicates such a sense of excitement about his art, and such a sense of wonder about the gift that is his extraordinary voice. "The thrill of performing hasn't changed in years," he says, "I learn something different every day. I've never gotten bored yet and I don't think I ever will."

Anthony Dominick Benedetto was born in Astoria, Queens. He is an eight-time Grammy winner and has released ninety-eight albums to date. Tony Bennett enjoys a flourishing second career as an accomplished painter and has exhibited his work in galleries around the world.

I GREW UP DURING the Depression. My father died when I was ten and my mother raised all three of us while she worked as a seamstress. On Sundays all of our relatives would come for dinner and after the meal they would form a circle around us kids and we would entertain them. Those Sundays singing with my family inspired me to become a performer, and after fifty years I love to sing as much as when I was a child. During the Depression all eyes were on President Roosevelt. He created a sense of community and renewed hope for those who had lost faith in the American Dream. When I was growing up he represented to many Americans their only hope for the future.

I also witnessed the inspiring example of Dr. Martin Luther King Jr., who, like Franklin D. Roosevelt, knew the importance of words. Another political leader I admire is Mario Cuomo, whom I met many years ago in front of the Hyatt Hotel in Manhattan. I walked up to him and said, "Sir, my name's Tony Bennett and I'm a singer." But before I could finish my introduction he beamed and said, "Boulevard of Broken Dreams," which was my first single. Cuomo, a humanitarian like Roosevelt and King, has the unique ability to bring diverse people together. I think he is able to accomplish this because he has that special gift of understanding government's responsibility to those in need. It is no surprise to me that Mario Cuomo also grew up in the Depression and has likely benefited from the same Roosevelt policies that I did. His message, again like Roosevelt and Martin Luther King, spoke to a better world and each citizen's responsibility to help build a better America.

There was a common thread through each of these individuals: an appreciation for who we are and who we can become. They helped me understand this and inspire all of us to fight apathy, to fully participate in the democratic process, and assume a personal stake in the well-being of our world.

These three distinguished men are my role models. They demonstrate that the American Dream is still alive.

BILL BRADLEY

SENATE PHOTO STUDIO

As a U.S. senator from New Jersey (1979–97), Bill Bradley made important contributions on key legislation and issues, including tax reform, international trade, pension reform, community building, and race relations. He was the chief author of the 1992 Freedom Exchange Act, an educational exchange initiative with the countries of the former Soviet Union, and the Omnibus Water Bill of 1992, which overhauled the California Central Valley Project, the nation's largest water project. Before becoming a U.S. senator, Bradley was a basketball star who played for the New York Knicks.

ONE PERSON OUTSIDE MY FAMILY who played a significant role in my life and who served as my mentor was Ed Macauley, a former basketball player in the National Basketball Association. At a lecture on basketball which I attended when I was fourteen, he said, "If you're not practicing, remember, someone else somewhere is practicing, and given roughly equal ability, if you two meet, he will win." His words stayed with me and gave me the incentive to work endlessly on my game.

This experience gave me a perspective on the game I loved. My parents could not really provide this because they did not have much informed interest in basketball and therefore could not share my passion for playing.

Ed helped me to establish work habits in every area of my life—habits that last a lifetime, for as my wife says, Ed's lesson is the origin of my workaholism.

James Brady

MURRAY BOGNOVITZ

In 1981, James Brady achieved his ultimate goal when he was appointed by President Ronald Reagan to be his assistant and the White House press secretary. However, his service was interrupted when John Hinckley attempted to assassinate President Reagan and shot him, Mr. Brady, and two officers. Though seriously wounded, Brady was able to continue as the White House press secretary until Reagan left office.

Since leaving the White House, Mr. Brady has spent time lobbying with his wife, Sarah Brady, the chair of Handgun Control, Inc., for stronger gun laws. On November 30, 1993, President Bill Clinton signed into law the "Brady Bill," which requires a national waiting period and background check on all handgun purchases. Mr. Brady also serves on the board of trustees of the Center to Prevent Handgun Violence.

JAMES BRADY

James Brady was born in Centralia, Illinois. He graduated from the University of Illinois, where he earned a B.S. in communications and political science.

MY MOTHER, DOROTHY BRADY, first involved me in politics and the Boy Scouts. She was the first female elected to the position of precinct committeeman of the state of Illinois.

Her primary responsibilities included voter registration and transporting voters to the polls—she would pick them up at their houses and drive them there. It was an early lesson in organization for me. She had everything accounted for and always emphasized the importance of organization.

My mom got me involved in the Boy Scouts, where I eventually became a Distinguished Eagle Scout. For me, it was an early start in doing good deeds and putting other people before myself, because scouting is about helping people and accomplishing goals through teamwork. My mom was a certified social worker who instilled in me the importance of community service and involvement. She also encouraged me to enter all types of contests. Whether at the local, state, or national level, she would tell me to get an entry form. It didn't matter whether I was good at what the contest called for, it was important just to enter and try one's best to succeed. It was a great educational experience that benefited me throughout my personal and professional career.

My father was six-foot-two and a yardmaster for the Burlington Railroad (also called the Q by railroad people). He put trains together to be filled at the coal mines in Cessar and Waltonville, Illinois. They would join one hundred hopper cars in the rail yard and take the trains to the mines to be filled with coal, then the coal would go all over the country. The Southern Rail also came through our town on its way to the mines.

If my dad knew the engineer, he would occasionally take me on the train to the mines. We would ride in the big steam-powered locomotives, this being the days before the diesel locomotives. We would travel up to Waltonville and my dad would tell me all sorts of train trivia and history as he talked with the engineer. He knew all the locomotives: their features, history, and evolution. We would watch the coal being loaded tender by tender until they filled the water tank, and then we'd travel back home.

My father taught me the lesson of hard work. He would get up at 4:30 A.M., fix his own breakfast, and walk to work. He would always rather walk than drive.

I knew when he would get off work and I would wait for him by the tracks. We would walk home together and he would tell me all that had happened at the rail yard that day.

My mother somehow saw to it that I was employed by Senate Majority Leader Everett McKinley Dirksen, of Illinois. In my precollege days I served as an aide on his staff. My job consisted of serving as a liaison between Mr. Dirksen and the Illinois county fair administrators. At every county fair, each political group was designated a particular night for their representatives to speak. On Republican night, for instance, the Republican candidates and politicians were expected to show up and speak at the fair. The same was granted for the Democrats. If the politicians didn't speak in certain counties, it was their political death sentence. My job was to meet with the county fair representatives and smooth things over if Mr. Dirksen was going to miss a particular fair. It wasn't always a fun job, but I learned a great deal about the importance of communicating with your constituents.

I went to the University of Illinois at Champain-Urbana, where I became active in government as a student senator. I had learned to set up a campaign from my mother, who taught, of course, that political success all came down to organization. I found that her system worked in student campaigns and, as I later discovered, in state and national campaigns as well.

On an airplane, certain gauges show that you are in the air. For the plane to be moving, the needles on those gauges have to be moving. I've always tried to focus on movement, on getting that gauge to show that you are flying, because if the needle isn't moving, you're not going anywhere.

I still feel my mom pushing me to keep going forward. It's probably a combination of my mother, father, and God. My mom probably has heaven organized by now. I'm sure it was organized before, but not Dorothy D. Brady organized.

Our time on earth can go two ways: it can be like putting your hand in a bucket of water or leaving a solid impression. When you put your hand in the water it only makes a ripple. There's no impression. I've always tried to make an impression, for which I credit my parents.

Helen Gurley Brown

FRANCESCO SCAVULLO

Helen Gurley Brown was born in Green Forest, Arkansas. In 1962, she wrote *Sex and the Single Girl,* which became a bestseller and remained on bestseller lists everywhere well into 1963. The book was published in twenty-eight countries and translated into sixteen languages. Her other books include *Sex and the Office,* also a bestseller, and *The Outrageous Opinions of Helen Gurley Brown.*

In 1965, Mrs. Brown became editor in chief of *Cosmopolitan* magazine, and the rest is publishing history. Today there are thirty-six international editions of the magazine. As of 1997, Mrs. Brown serves as editor in chief of all foreign-language versions.

Mrs. Brown was inducted into the Publisher's Hall of Fame in 1988. She is, in her own words, "a health nut, a feminist, an irredeemable but contented workaholic, and passionately interested in the relationship between men and women."

I WAS BORN IN GREEN FOREST, Arkansas (population three hundred), grew up in Little Rock, and moved to Los Angeles as a teenager. My mother, Cleo Gurley, was the earliest influence in my life, and her encouragement was vital to me both as a child and an adult. Like my father, Ira Gurley, she was a teacher. Unlike my father, she was what you call an early feminist, while he voted against women's suffrage. He asked her not to work after they were married, declaring that no wife of his would work, although they could have used the money and she loved her job.

She quit teaching and fairly soon gave birth to her first baby, my sister Mary, and then me. She poured all the energy she had given to teaching into raising Mary and myself.

My parents were intelligent; both had attended college, my father graduating from law school, and I inherited their love of learning. Like my mother, my father encouraged me to be the best at anything I tried. I remember his helping me, paragraph by paragraph, write an essay for a school contest entitled "What Cotton Means to Me." I was nine years old. My father died when I was ten and, quite naturally, my mother became the main influence in my life.

Her guidance was quite different in the ways most mothers of that era influenced their daughters. By frequently warning me through the years not to get married and have children too soon, she emphasized the importance of using my intelligence. With her encouragement, I ran for student government, participated in any contest I could find, and tried out for school plays. I really can't say she was a role model, since she was never able to fulfill her potential in her career, but she was definitely a mentor, someone I looked up to and tried to please.

All this time I was growing up, little girls were supposed to be cute—little princesses, curly-haired, and preferably blonde. Although my mother wanted my sister and me to look nice and spent a mountain of time making our clothes on her trusty Singer sewing machine, she never failed to emphasize the development of the mind, beaming at good report cards and helping with our homework if requested.

In high school a bad case of acne was the blight of my life, but my mother helped me move beyond this scourge. Rather than becoming a recluse, I gathered the courage to be outgoing, involving myself in activities even more and making friends.

Throughout school, a few teachers recognized my writing talent but no one had the same overwhelming impact on me as my mother. Writing stories and poetry and keeping a diary were interests that she encouraged.

After high school I didn't have too many choices for the future—money was scarce. After graduating (president of the Scholarship Society, class valedictorian—Cleo's influence!) I attended business college for a few months to learn to type and take shorthand. I paid my tuition by working for an announcer at KHJ, a radio station. Salary: $6.00 per week. After that, I had jobs at many different corporations working as a secretary.

Not being able to send me to college broke my mother's heart, but she always encouraged me to work hard at whatever I was doing, not just because we needed the money—she never pushed that aspect of my work—but because she wanted me to use my brain. I don't know if she would have wanted me to take it this far, but, through the years, I have always enjoyed work more than play. Yes, it's brought money, but more importantly, recognition and satisfaction.

At age thirty-six I met my husband, David Brown, who turned out to be another important mentor. When I was having a bit of a shaky time in my copywriting job, I asked if he could think of a book I might write and he suggested that I write about being single. That book became *Sex and the Single Girl*. It was a big bestseller and on the *New York Times* bestseller list for six months.

We never expected such a reaction but were thrilled when it happened. So much mail poured in from young women that David suggested I start a magazine and answer everyone at one time. The two of us put together a format and he took it all over New York but did not find a publisher. However, he interested the Hearst Corporation in letting us try our format on its once illustrious, but then failing, *Cosmopolitan*.

The corporation gave me a year to make good, but the magazine took off with our first issue. David was never coeditor, but, there wouldn't have been any "new Cosmo" if he hadn't helped me sell the idea to a publisher and if he hadn't continued to be involved with its publication for the thirty-two years I was editor in chief. He wrote the cover blurbs for every single issue during my reign.

We all have different types of friends—girl, boy, work, social—and sometimes they overlap. But I would hope everyone has at least one friend who can help him or her in a career. *Mentor* is a rather heavy-sounding word, implying a serious commitment, but a mentor can simply be someone you go to for advice, talk over ideas with, or share your hopes, dreams, and ambitions. All you need is a friend who is interested in you and your career, who knows a lot about the professional world you are in or hope to get into, and will be there to offer guidance and advice.

ARTHUR CALIANDRO

STEVE TORRES © MARBLE COLLEGIATE CHURCH

Each Sunday, Dr. Arthur Caliandro draws overflow crowds to services in the nineteenth-century Marble Church sanctuary at 29th Street and Fifth Avenue, in New York. His practical sermons, peppered with humor and enhanced with down-home, self-effacing storytelling, are a source of weekly inspiration.

Marble Church became world-renowned when Norman Vincent Peale spread the message of the power of positive thinking from its pulpit. In October 1984, Dr. Caliandro succeeded Dr. Peale, becoming the forty-sixth senior minister in a tradition that began in 1628.

Since 1967, Dr. Caliandro has motivated the congregation of Marble Church to participate in outreach programs involving hundreds of volunteers in helping disadvantaged children, the homeless, the hospitalized, those with acquired immune deficiency syndrome (AIDS), and other communities in crisis. In cooperation with a Jewish temple and a Catholic parish, Marble helped found Manhattan's Tri-Faith Shelter for Homeless Men. It also sponsors Help Line, the largest crisis-intervention telephone service in the country. And, following a philosophy of compassion and empowerment, Marble became the first church to adopt an "I Have a Dream" class, promising to support dozens of young Harlem students through college.

I AM VERY FORTUNATE to have had a mentor. My life and career have been profoundly affected by the interest, wisdom, and affirmation of someone who believed in me. My way of thanking him is to position myself to do for others what he did for me.

This very special man was Amos Parrish. I was told that for nearly thirty years he was one of the top marketing geniuses in the United States. His mind was so keen, his intuitive sense so alert, that William Sarnoff, the founder of NBC, used him as a personal consultant.

I met Amos when he was seventy-eight and I was a young minister of thirty-five. He had heard me preach a few times and obviously was aware that I needed a lot of help. He invited me to lunch at the University Club in New York and said, "I like you. I think I can help you." Then he added, "Would you mind if I adopted you?"

I had no idea what was going on. It was an awkward moment for me because I didn't know this man well and really was unaware of how much help I needed. Nevertheless, I went along with his interest in helping me. For nearly five years we met every other Tuesday at the same table of the University Club.

There are few things more important that any human being can experience than the sincere affirmation of another significant person. Amos Parrish seemed to believe in me and feel I could really be effective. I gained great encouragement in my dreams of achieving and making my life count. Some of the lessons I learned are still in my consciousness today. At one of our luncheons he said, "Arthur, you must deal with big ideas." When I asked him what a big idea was, he responded, "A big idea is one that challenges people, stretches their minds, and brings them to bigger and better places." Ever since then I have been aware of how much we deal with small-minded and petty thinking and behavior, and I have tried to avoid it in myself.

I also learned an enormous amount about perspective from him. Once when he was in his early nineties and commenting on some current event, he said, "You know, Arthur, when we're in the midst of something we really see very little of all that is going on. It is only after the fact that we understand and see what happened." This was very humbling for me because I learned not to be too self-assured and cocky when I thought I might have an edge on understanding something.

When he was in his middle eighties, Amos moved to Tucson. Our relationship continued, sometimes by telephone and visits, but mostly through the mail. In longhand he wrote pages and pages of his reflections on life, motivation, loving, changing, and the like. It was a wise, experienced older man pouring himself into a younger man just starting out.

He was born at the time the first automobile was invented and lived to see man land on the moon. He also had an enormous respect for the creative ability of the human being—he was big on awe. I remember walking down Park Avenue with him one day when he stopped at a giant skyscraper. "Look up," he cried. "The sheer size of that building will keep you humble." In the same vein, while visiting him in Tucson, one night as we looked at the setting sun over the mountains, he said, "Just think. That same sunset has been happening for ten million years."

He told many stories about relationships, those that worked and those that didn't. I learned that a good relationship is like a work of art, and based upon a good attitude, a patient and listening ear, and a lot of empathy, understanding, and forgiveness. He believed in forgiveness. He couldn't understand why any person would hold a grudge or seek revenge.

Time and again I have heard of the mentor and the person mentored running into conflict which ruptured the relationship.

This is usually more hurtful to the mentor than to the younger person. I can see how it happens—the younger person begins to feel a new strength and a desire for independence. I am glad to say this never happened between Amos Parrish and me.

He died at ninety-two of acute leukemia. Knowing he would go rather quickly, I was on alert for several weeks so I could fly out to Arizona and spend a day with him. One night his daughter called and asked, "Can you come tomorrow?"

He knew he was dying, and I knew it, but he chose not to talk about it. We spent that day together reflecting on life and talking about big ideas—awe and love.

Today he continues to mentor me—his outpouring of self is deeply rooted in my consciousness. Much of what I am about is influenced by much of what Amos Parrish was about.

ROGER CARAS

Naturalist Roger S. Caras, a prolific author and broadcast correspondent on animals, wildlife, and the environment became president of the American Society for the Prevention of Cruelty to Animals in 1991. He directs its policy and is a source of knowledge, experience, compassion, and perspective in an often volatile field. Caras believes that humane advocacy is best accomplished when lines of communication are kept open with those holding differing views.

Born in 1928 in Methuen, Massachusetts, Caras has logged over seven million miles of air travel as a broadcaster on radio and television networks. His writing has appeared in scores of books, newspapers, and magazines. He has also lectured throughout the world.

WHEN I WAS SIXTEEN I was kicked out of high school for being uneducatable. I had extremely low self-esteem—it seemed to be my father's life work to have me that way—and was sent to Huntington School for Boys, a private school in Boston.

My English teacher at Huntington, Rowland Leach, was an interesting character. Mr. Leach was not a cuddly man. When you first saw him you did not think to yourself, here is a man I want to walk up to and hug.

Yet despite all his gruffness, he was an immensely warm man who really cared about his job and his students. He was the type of teacher who wanted you to love what he taught as much as he did. But, of course, it was all on his terms. That's what made him unique. He always was offering innovative approaches to the subject matter of his classes. One semester he warned that no one could pass his English class without seeing Lawrence Olivier's film *Henry V.*

He saw my needs and offered a great deal of encouragement. He helped me to believe in myself, and made a world of difference. My studies became more focused and my self-esteem skyrocketed.

In 1961, fifteen years after I saw Mr. Leach for the last time, I published my first book and proudly sent him a copy with a lengthy personal inscription. When I didn't hear back from this teacher that I respected so much, I was hurt. I felt he should have acknowledged my accomplishment. Just when I was going to send him another copy, I got a package from him. Inside was my book. He had returned it to me corrected and graded. He gave me a pretty good mark, too. He was quite a character.

Mr. Leach also encouraged my love of film. It was through his guidance that I began viewing it as an art form, and after graduating from high school I went on to pursue a degree in film from the University of Southern California.

At USC I was lucky enough to be taught by Andreas Deinum, a Dutch film theorist. I loved that man. He and his wife were the most caring people in the world. Because of him, I experienced growth in both my personal life and studies. While they were traveling in Europe, he was named before the House of Representatives Un-American Activities Committee and blacklisted. Returning to USC, he was promptly fired. He got a teaching position at the University of Oregon, where he later suffered a heart attack.

What struck me most about Mr. Leach was that he was so utterly human. He cared for others and was intolerant of any form of idiocy or injustice. I found it shattering to see him powerless at the hands of those who were so hypocritical. The McCarthy era was a sad time for this country.

I was working as a volunteer in the herpetology department at Harvard University for a person I did not get along with, but there was another scientist a few doors down from me whose specialty was butterflies and moths. He would make little displays of specimens for me and I would take the cases to the library to research and learn about them. The name of this specialist was Vladimir Nabokov. Many people don't know that he was not only a writer but a scientist.

I also had the good fortune to know and work with Stanley Kubrick. Late one Sunday night, Stanley called and wanted me to join him and the science fiction writer Arthur C. Clarke for a very late supper. I replied that I was not one of those fancy Hollywood types who could sleep until three in the afternoon, I had to go to work. Stanley told me that I should call in and quit the next morning. He and Arthur were about to go to England to begin work on a project tentatively titled *2001: A Space Odyssey.* (He was sure that Metro-Goldwyn-Mayer would never allow them to keep this title.) With my wife's approval, I quit my job of ten years at Columbia Pictures and we moved to England for three years to work on that monumental film.

I have been extremely fortunate in my life and career. I have been a devoted follower of the High Priestess Serendipity and did whatever she has suggested I do. It has benefited my life immensely.

If you read an autobiography, you simply read of one person's relationship in a series of relationships. That's exactly what makes up a life. It's one relationship after another. If you don't have those friendships, you won't have much else that matters.

Elaine Chao

An Asian immigrant who came to the United States when she was eight, Chao earned an undergraduate degree from Mount Holyoke College and an M.B.A. from Harvard University. Since 1992, she has served as president and CEO of the United Way of America, the 108-year-old organization that serves two thousand United Way chapters across the country. After the federal government, the United Way supports the greatest variety of health and human services in the country. Chao also served as head of the Federal Maritime Commission, deputy secretary of the U.S. Department of Transportation, and executive director of the Peace Corps. In 1991, President George Bush appointed her to head the Peace Corps, which made its first foray into Eastern Europe during her tenure. Chao is married to U.S. Senator Mitch McConnell of Kentucky.

As an American of Asian descent who grew up in a family of daughters, I am fortunate to have had parents who believed deeply in the Lord and who instilled within their children the empowering philosophy that life held many possibilities if we worked hard, developed discipline, and set goals. My parents are incredibly inspiring people. When I was five years old, my father went to America to seek a better life with greater opportunities. It was not until I was eight years old that he was able to send for us to join him.

My father was my primary mentor. He encouraged me at every turn throughout my childhood. In my early career days, too, I often turned to him for advice and counsel. He never told me exact answers to specific questions. Rather, he helped tease out certain principles and then encouraged me to think through the problem myself. He often said, "If I only help you solve your immediate challenge, and not help you understand the underlying principle this particular challenge entailed, you will never learn to resolve situations on your own. I can only help you understand general principles. From these principles, you can face hosts of challenges and situations on your own."

Every Saturday morning when we were growing up, my father would rouse the children out of bed and we would be given our Saturday cleaning chores. In the afternoon, he would work around the house, fixing the plumbing, pipes, or other odds and ends. One of his daughters would accompany him, ostensibly to be his assistant. We held the flashlight or handed him his tools as he worked on the pipes. During these chores, he would tell us about his childhood and what China was like when he was growing up. Later in life, I found his stories empowering and inspiring.

My close relationship with my father gave me a strong sense of self-esteem. Indeed, my optimistic view of the future is due primarily to his influence. As a young man, he came to America speaking poor, accented English. He suffered from discrimination and financial hardship, but never lost faith in God or in America.

He believed that individuals could shape their own destinies. He never saw himself as a victim.

Because of my father's immigrant history, my parents and I have always felt strongly about our obligation to contribute to society. At a very young age, I remember my father reminding us to be a credit to our community and to lend a helping hand to others. These beliefs influenced me in my job choices, for I decided to work for the federal government and nonprofit organizations as a professional volunteer.

I hope people take the time to be mentors, to share themselves with others. It will be one of the most fulfilling and enriching experiences of their lives, and our communities and country will ultimately be better for their participation.

JULIA CHILD

MICHAEL MCLAUGHLIN

Julia Child was born in Pasadena, California, and graduated from Smith College in 1934. After World War II, her husband Paul was assigned to the U.S. Information Service at the American Embassy in Paris. It was there that she started her culinary career by enrolling at the Cordon Bleu cooking school.

After she was given a television interview at WGBH in Boston, *The French Chef* was launched on February 11, 1963. Following that success, she branched out into contemporary cuisine with the series *Julia Child and Company, Julia Child and More Company,* and *Dinner at Julia's.* Her newest television venture is a twenty-two-part series with Jacques Pepin. The series offers a technique-based program aimed at teaching the serious home cook. It will air in the fall of 1999.

Julia Child's books include *The French Chef Cookbook, Mastering the Art of French Cooking, I* and *II,* and numerous other cookbooks.

THE FIRST INFLUENTIAL FIGURE in my life was my grade-school English teacher, Carolyn P. Adams. She was a fine, fair woman who loved children. She instilled in me a respect for others and made me want to really listen to people. Over the years I've found that it is only by listening to others that you can leave yourself open to learning.

I really didn't start cooking until I was married. My husband and I traveled to Europe soon afterward. While visiting Paris I became fascinated with French cuisine. It was so different from anything I had tasted in the United States and boasted a long tradition. In Europe, cooking is a revered art form. American cooking was different than European cooking, at least in how it was perceived at that time.

Returning to the United States, I began studying the classic French cookbooks written by the French master chefs. I followed the texts of Escoffier and Caesar Ritz, who worked with Escoffier at his hotel in Paris. Their writing and cuisine inspired my career. I published my own cookbook, *Mastering the Art of French Cooking*, and began a cooking show on public television when a news show wanted to inject some art and culture into its programming. They decided to have cooking on the show, and I agreed to give cooking demonstrations. The segments became so popular that we started our own show, which enjoyed great success because French cooking was beginning to become fashionable in the United States. It became a status symbol, food and wine were signs that someone had "arrived."

A lot of this new visibility resulted from technological progress, with Europe becoming more accessible because of air travel. It used to take days to travel by boat across the Atlantic. Then airplanes took only a few hours and were more affordable. This, and the fact that the economy in the years following World War II was for the most part prosperous, allowed more Americans to travel. Traveling became less about privilege and more about culture.

There are those who say that no one cooks anymore or even wants to learn. But everywhere I go, cooking classes are filled to capacity. It's really wonderful. I'm constantly busy, and my work keeps me young. Lately I've been writing at the computer and working on a new television series with Jacques Pepin. We are in the process of taping twenty-two shows for the series *Just Cooking*. I love my work and know how lucky I am.

I'm in a good profession that young people should get involved in. There are many rewards to cooking; it's not just about the final product. For me, it's just as much about the process. And if you love your work, you can go anywhere with it.

Bon Apetit!

TIMOTHY GREENFIELD-SANDERS

KENNETH COLE

Footwear and accessory designer Kenneth Cole founded his company, Kenneth Cole Productions, in December 1982. Today, the company manufactures internationally and distributes men's and women's footwear and accessories under the labels Kenneth Cole, Reaction, and Unlisted, besides offering over thirty products through various licensing partners.

Kenneth Cole's controversial advertising campaign has garnered worldwide attention for its humor and social consciousness. In 1985, he was the first member of the fashion community to take a public stand in the fight against acquired immunodeficiency syndrome (AIDS). Since then, he has continued to support the global fight through both personal and corporate initiatives, including the dedication of an ongoing portion of his marketing budget to public awareness initiatives. Cole serves as a national board member of AmFAR, the American Foundation for AIDS research, and the HELP USA homeless project.

Kenneth Cole Productions continues to declare, "What you stand for is more important than what you stand in" and "To be aware is more important than what you wear."

MY FATHER, CHARLES COLE, would wake me up at 5:00 many Saturday mornings, starting when I was ten. He would invite me into his world, a world that he didn't share with many people. At 5:30 we would have breakfast and talk about what was happening in my world. Then we would go to his shoe factory in lower Manhattan, and I would sit with him in his office and watch him as he worked.

He served in the marines in World War II and was stationed in the South Pacific. He was a tough guy, very strong willed, and a hands-on businessman. He would be in the factory opening cartons and in the office opening mail. He knew each step of the manufacturing process and what was written on every piece of paper.

He was very much of the "do as I do" mentality, not only to me but to all of the people who worked there. He inspired everyone around him and took a personal interest in the lives of all the people he worked with. His passion for business was not that much different than his approach to everything in his life.

In the early 1970s I went to Emory University in Atlanta for my undergraduate degree with the intention of attending law school. As I was about to embark on my legal education, my father's right-hand man left the factory to start a competitive business.

To help my father, I put off law school to learn the business as quickly as I could. I knew that in order to succeed I would need the support and respect of everyone in the company, including my father, but not having enough experience and knowledge, I realized I couldn't impress them with the quality of my work. So I set out to show them what I could with the quantity of my work. If the first worker arrived at 6:30 A.M., I would arrive at 6:15.

I found myself fascinated with the production process from beginning to end. I seemed to always gravitate to the sample room, where the product was designed and manufactured, understanding that this was the nucleus of the business. Then I would find the time to help open the mail or sweep the floor.

I became fascinated with the concept of transforming an idea into a new style of shoe. With my father's encouragement, I took it upon myself to create my own collection of footwear, different from anything the factory had ever made. Open to creative alternatives and anxious to further encourage me, my dad then suggested I visit the principle industry publication, *Footwear News,* and on the way back bring the samples to some important buyers. *Footwear News* proceeded to write a story in the next edition about a new up-and-coming designer, and each customer who saw the shoes bought some. I was off and running.

I loved that the rewards for those efforts were so quick in coming and that there were no specific rules. I realized that if I had chosen to study the law, I would always be judged by my legal knowledge in contrast to what I was doing, where no rules existed. I knew that the further I went beyond what had been done before, the more likely I would succeed.

Over the next five years my father and I built a successful business together. I then realized that I needed to take on the ultimate challenge of starting my own business. I did it confidently with his encouragement and never looked back. I was lucky that so early in my career I had such a great role model who gave me the tools to be successful, the practical experience on how to use them, and the courage to trust my instincts.

I made great strides in a very competitive field, but I reached a point when it all started to become a little empty. I needed to find a way to make things more relevant. I knew that if I were going to continue to give so much of myself I would have to find a way to make it part of something bigger. So early on in the company's development I decided to make the awareness of meaningful social issues an important part of the company's culture, so that "what one stands for is more important than what they stand in," and that "to be aware is more important than what you wear." These principles would eventually become part of the company's philosophy.

My father, my mentor, by his example, was a testament of the value of hard work and the concern for one's fellow human beings. He did everything with all of his heart as well as his "sole."

ARTHUR ELGORT

CINDY CRAWFORD

Cindy Crawford is one of the most recognizable faces in the world, having appeared on over four hundred magazine covers throughout Europe and the United States. She recently took on a new challenge by writing her first book, *Cindy Crawford's Basic Face,* a makeup workbook published by Broadway Books.

She crossed over from the world of fashion and beauty to the arena of broadcast journalism as host of MTV's *House of Style* for six years. She has also produced several successful exercise videos and guest hosted ABC's morning talk show *Regis and Kathie Lee* and NBC's late night show, *Later.*

In October 1995 Crawford made her acting debut opposite William Baldwin in Warner Brothers's action-adventure film *Fair Game,* produced by Joel Silver.

Born and raised in DeKalb, Illinois, Crawford has become one of the most successful models of all time. She is well-known for her annual calendars and as an international spokesperson for Revlon. She divides her time between New York and Los Angeles.

I HAVE BEEN BLESSED throughout my life by encountering people who have enabled me to grow and develop as an individual.

First and foremost, my mother has always given me her unconditional love and support. She has always had great faith in me and with her inherent strength of character she challenged me to fulfill my dreams. Even during her divorce with my father she had a positive outlook on life. She explained to me that when you try your best there is no failure: "You can always come home again. Failure is when you do not try at all."

My father also had a great deal of influence on me. He inspired me to be ambitious and to develop a love of learning. He also challenged me and consistently emphasized that girls could accomplish as much, or more, than boys.

I was fortunate to have great teachers every year in school. In the fourth grade I had a student teacher determined to confer nicknames on her students. I was dubbed "Future Miss America." She helped me to understand that beyond the confines of my hometown there was a whole world of possibilities to explore.

Mr. Halvorson, my high school calculus teacher, was an exceptional person. I appreciated the fact that he was both an authority figure and a friend. He emphasized that the world is a bigger place than our familiar neighborhood. He filled his students with excitement and anticipation for the future. Mr. Halvorson also taught me a strong lesson—that learning can be fun.

Looking back on my career, I realize that modeling has changed throughout the years and that I have been a real part of that change. In Chicago, a photographer, Victor Skrebneski, stands out among the myriad of people that have affected this important facet of my life. At the age of eighteen he recognized my potential and gave me counseling that would last a lifetime. First, he told me to regard modeling as a profession and a job, not a lifestyle. Second, he told me that my job as a model was to make the clothes of the client look as good as possible. When Victor taught me that modeling was a job and "not about me" I was realistic about the career path I was undertaking.

When I was twenty I decided to move to New York City to further my career. I was already equipped with valuable tools and lessons that would serve me well. My job skills included discipline, being on time, and doing the best work I could. Payment was commensurate to the quality of performance.

I have been fortunate to know extraordinary individuals who have consistently been strong influences on my life. They have challenged me and empowered me to develop my talents and become successful. I cannot remember a year when I did not have their sage counsel and encouragement when needed. All of these wonderful people enabled me to be who I am today.

Walter Cronkite

STEVE FRIEDMAN © 1996 CBS

Walter Cronkite has covered virtually every major news event during his more than sixty years in journalism—the last forty-eight affiliated with CBS News. He became a special correspondent for CBS News on March 6, 1981, when he stepped down as anchorman and managing editor of the *CBS Evening News* after nearly nineteen years in that role.

A sampling of Cronkite's assignments for CBS News over three decades reads like a synopsis of American and world history—exclusive interviews with most major heads of state, including all U.S. presidents since Harry S Truman; all aspects of the American political scene since 1952, including Watergate; and newsmaking events around the world, including the events surrounding the siege of the American Embassy in Iran and the Vietnam War. Cronkite's unflappability under pressure inspired the affectionate nickname of Old Iron Pants, while his accomplishments earned him acclaim from his journalism colleagues, other professionals, and the American public.

I WENT TO SAN JACINTO HIGH SCHOOL in Houston, Texas, in the 1930s and was fortunate to come in contact with a man who would inspire me to become a career print and broadcast journalist. Fred Birney was a pioneer in high school journalism. Very few high schools at that time even taught journalism, and many schools didn't have their own student newspaper.

Fred talked the Houston Board of Education into allowing him to teach a journalism class once a week at three local high schools, one of which was San Jacinto. He was a newspaperman of the old school and taught us a great deal about reporting and writing. He also became a sponsor of the San Jacinto High School newspaper, the *Campus Cub*. Under his tutelage, we published it monthly, whereas it had previously been published in a casual manner, just three or four times a year. During my junior year, I was the sports editor of the *Campus Cub* and its chief editor in my senior year.

Fred was a hands-on technical teacher, explaining the complexities of layout and copy. He also stressed the importance of the tight lead—the diminished inverted pyramid of an article's development and the necessity of taking an honest approach toward the subject matter.

At the time, I was an avid reader of *American Boy Magazine*, which was composed of a series of short stories to inspire boys to follow certain careers. I remember reading an article about mining engineers. I wish I had read an article about petroleum engineering in Texas in the 1930s instead of becoming interested in mineral mining. So here I was about to graduate, and I was torn between becoming a mining engineer and a journalist. Things could have been a lot different for me without Fred.

He was well-connected with the three newspapers in Houston. During the summer of my junior year, he secured his interested students jobs as copy boys and girls with the *Houston Post.* Then, after I graduated in 1933, I became the campus correspondent for the *Houston Post* at the University of Texas at Austin and worked at the college paper, the *Daily Texan,* working my way up to become its editor. My sophomore year I got a weekend job working as an exalted copy boy for the *International News Service* at the state capitol, but I was also asked to cover committee meetings of the state legislature.

That same year I was hired as a full-time cub reporter with the Scripps Howard Bureau, where I was taken under the wing of another newsman, Vann Kennedy. He gave me a great deal of advice and tutelage, and many chances to cover stories at the capitol.

Texas politics was an interesting arena for a budding journalist because the state legislative committee meetings addressed a number of special interest areas: farming, timber, cotton, mining, and many others. All these groups lobbied the various politicians to advance their own legislative self-interests.

At this time the country was in a time of immense transition. Technology was advancing at a rapid rate, and the money generated by these special interest groups, especially in Texas, was growing rapidly. It was an exciting time to be covering politics at any level.

At the end of my sophomore year, I was offered a job as a full-time reporter at the *Houston Press.* Roy Roussel was the city editor and his brother Peter was the culture editor. They helped me a great deal and I learned a lot from them. I was with the *Press* for a year and a half and never returned to college.

I was visiting my grandparents in Kansas City in 1936 when I saw an ad in the *Kansas City Star* for a radio station broadcasting football games in Oklahoma. Radio was new at the time and it was an exciting opportunity; it was in its primitive stages then—we got the news straight off the wire service. So I applied for the job and was hired to cover University of Oklahoma football games and news for WKY in Oklahoma City. However, the job lacked the excitement of my previous reporting experience.

I covered football until the threat of war became more of a reality. It was then that I realized my need to get back into news reporting. I was hired by the United Press, where I stayed for eleven years and served as a war correspondent during World War II. In 1950 I was hired by CBS and became further involved in radio and television.

Fred Birney wouldn't admire the type of journalism going on today. He was always big on journalistic integrity. "You've got to remember that everyone you write about is a human being," he would tell us, "not just a headline."

We exchanged several letters until his death, shortly after my high school graduation. He taught me so much in those high school classes, and by securing me those early jobs, he cemented my desire to be a reporter for the rest of my life. He was my major inspiration. I always credit Fred Birney for my career.

ANDREW CUOMO

Andrew Cuomo has served as U.S. Secretary of Housing and Urban Development since January 1997. He has reinvented the Department with historic management reforms to make it more efficient and effective. Secretary Cuomo has led successful efforts to improve public housing, increase rental assistance subsidies for poor families, boost America's homeownership rate to an all-time high, reduce housing discrimination, revitalize urban America, and expand programs for homeless Americans.

Cuomo came to HUD in 1993 as an Assistant Secretary. In 1987, Cuomo founded HELP USA (Housing Enterprise for the Less Privileged), the nation's largest private provider of transitional housing for the homeless. Earlier, Cuomo served as a top aide to his father, New York Governor Mario M. Cuomo (accepting a salary of only $1 a year), as an Assistant District Attorney in Manhattan, and as a partner in a New York City law firm.

ANDREW CUOMO

Cuomo was born in New York City on December 6, 1957. He and his wife, Kerry Kennedy Cuomo, have three daughters. He is a graduate of Fordham University and Albany Law School.

OUR COUNTRY WAS BUILT by immigrants like my grandparents Andrea and Immaculata Cuomo and Charles and Mary Raffa. They came to this country because of the freedom of opportunity and the promise to provide a better life for their families. They helped me to understand that everyone deserves an opportunity to try their best for success. My grandparents were disciplined, self-sacrificing people who loved and wanted the best for their family. Though my grandfathers Charles and Andrea were born in the United States, they were raised in Italy, and returned to this country as adults. They believed that education was a gift that would give us the greatest strength: self-respect. And with self-respect we would become better citizens, better workers, better partners, better parents, and better human beings. They were especially proud to see their grandchildren furthering their learning. My grandparents were not highly educated, but they taught me and enriched my life by sharing many of life's lessons through anecdote and personal example.

As a youth, I recall the wonderful vacations spent at the Raffa summer home at Lake Hopatcong, New Jersey, and the barbecues at the Cuomo home in Holliswood, Queens. These were always happy events with swimming and boating and lots of food. Their hospitality and warmth made us feel that their homes were ours too, and that our friends were always welcome.

Holiday celebrations always took place at our house, and my parents maintained the traditions of our grandparents. And of course, my grandparents always participated in these festivities.

One experience I will never forget was when my beloved dog, Sport, was fatally injured by a speeding car. In addition to the loving care and understanding of my parents and siblings, it was Grandfather Andrea who made it easier for me to cope with my sorrow, by choosing a special burial site for Sport, in his backyard.

During my father's gubernatorial campaign, all the grandparents visited many senior citizen centers to speak on behalf of my father. Though they were wary of politics, they knew my father would be a good governor and would help people in need. Even in politics, family support made a big difference.

A few years ago, my wife Kerry and I traveled to Italy, and though I had visited Italy as a child, it was on that trip I recalled vividly and moreover, *understood,* the wonderful stories of my grandparents' Italy, the warmth of the Italian people, and the beauty of Italian culture and tradition.

Our wonderful grandparents left all of us—my sisters Margaret, Maria, and Madeline, my brother Christopher and me—with a legacy to be true to yourself and your ideals, and if you want to realize your potential and your dreams, a good education is the most important thing. I hope to leave these legacies to my own children. To my grandparents I say: You were the watchtower to my sisters, brother, and me. You were an extension of my parents, and we respect and love your for everything you did for our family. You helped us become the adults we are today. *Mille grazie!*

Mario M. Cuomo

Mario M. Cuomo began life in the struggling neighborhood of South Jamaica, Queens, at the height of the Great Depression. Though he could barely speak English when he began first grade in the New York City public schools, he graduated summa cum laude from St. John's University in Queens in 1953 and in 1956 tied for top-of-the-class honors at St. John's Law School.

He was elected New York State's fifty-second governor in 1982 and won reelection in 1986 and 1990. He was also the longest serving Democratic governor in the modern history of New York State and won the two largest electoral victories ever.

Since leaving public office, Governor Cuomo has returned to practicing law as a partner in the New York firm of Willkie, Farr & Gallagher, where he conducts a practice in national and international corporate law. In 1997, he became co-chairman and a member of the board of directors for the Partnership for a Drug-Free America. And in his most recent book, *Reason to Believe,* published in 1995, Governor Cuomo describes the challenges facing us today and points the way to workable answers.

The National Review has said this about the former governor: "Mario Cuomo has for years been hailed as both the philosopher-king and the humble "conscience' of the Democratic Party, a formidable, saintly genius of liberalism. Since his efflorescence at the 1984 Democratic convention, even many conservatives have accorded this, their archenemy, a certain respect."

BECAUSE I WAS BORN in the middle of the Depression, and my parents and older brother and sister were constantly occupied by our family grocery store and their jobs, I had an unusually spare relationship with the members of my family. All of them were bright, hard-working, loving, and generous people, and while we did not have all the time together we would have liked, their influence on me was all good and useful. Outside of my family there were few, if any, individuals who made lasting impressions on me. But there was the world of books.

Over the years, three different heroic figures had the greatest influence on me—Thomas More, Abraham Lincoln, and, of course, Jesus. In the case of More, I was impressed because he combined the law and public service and religious belief so well. And in the end, he put conscience over consequences to himself.

Lincoln's language fascinated me.

And Jesus offered me—and many millions of others—the best rationale for living.

Actually, these "mentors" intimidated me a bit because they were all so far beyond what I could ever be. But they set examples to admire and strive for. I wound up a lawyer in public life who is still struggling to learn to use language well, to put conscience over consequences, and to understand the world's basic rationale. All of this I have done very imperfectly, but better than I would have without my three role models.

The most valuable lesson my role models taught me is that the game is lost only when we stop trying for the greatest excellence of which we are capable. I'm still in the game.

OSSIE DAVIS

ANTHONY BARBOZA

Ossie Davis is well-known for his versatile roles and performances on and off Broadway, in films and on television, in addition to his roles as a writer, director, and public speaker. He is the recipient of many awards and citations, including an Emmy nomination and honorary degrees. In 1989, he was inducted into the Image Award Hall of Fame of the National Association for the Advancement of Colored People (NAACP) as well as the Broadway Hall of Fame.

His acting career began with the Rose McClendon Players in the basement of the 124th Street Library in Harlem. Since then, he has been featured in numerous film and television programs. Some of his recent film performances include *Doctor Doolittle, Twelve Angry Men, Grumpy Old Men, The Client,* and *Get On the Bus*. He has directed such films as *Cotton Comes to Harlem, Black Girl, Kongi's Harvest,* and *Countdown at Kusini.* The critically acclaimed series *With*

Ossie and Ruby, which he coproduced, is another impressive credit. His stage performances include *A Raisin in the Sun, Purlie Victorious,* which he wrote, and *I'm Not Rappaport.*

I GREW UP IN WAYCROSS, GEORGIA, and went to Center High School, where Mr. Lucius Jackson taught chemistry, physics, and coached several of the sports teams. In 1934, my parents moved to Valdosta, Georgia, but some of my teachers wanted me to finish my senior year at Central and graduate with my friends. They found a place for me to stay and allowed me to remain with my classmates that year.

Jack, as we called Lucius Jackson, was fond of me. I was a good student and smart enough to finish his chemistry courses a year early. Jack wanted me to go out for the football team but I felt that I wasn't big enough to play, and, temperamentally, I really wasn't a contact person—I didn't want to grab people or be grabbed by them. So he made me water boy and I went with the team everywhere.

I was also his laboratory assistant and helped teach the laboratory classes in chemistry. One day, an inquisitive and inventive friend of mine and I went to the lab to conduct our own experiment. We added the proper proportions of water, meal, and sugar until we had concocted a rather fine homebrew. Awaiting the time for fermentation to run its course, we ultimately took the proper scientific approach to such an experiment: we drank it. However, the principal at Central took exception to our scientific enthusiasm and wanted to kick us both out of school. Jack intervened on our behalf, saying he would be responsible for us the rest of the year.

Jack first put the idea of college in my mind, and prepared the proper mind-set for me to go to school. No one else in my family had gone to college—I would be the first.

I came to Harlem in April 1939 and found my way to the Rose McClendon Players, a local black acting company, where I first met Dick Campbell. He helped me get a job, a place to stay, and even lent me money. It was Dick Campbell who trained me, taking this raw country material and teaching "it" how to walk, talk, sit, stand—everything. More important, he taught me that theater and art were instrumental in the struggle of black people. We performed for the Urban League and at pageants for the NAACP. Theater and performance had a socially responsible aspect to them.

After World War II Dick became my agent and helped me land my first Broadway role by setting up an audition. After I got the part he helped negotiate my contract. He surrounded me with other actors who would keep an eye out for me and show me the tricks of the trade.

Both Lucius Jackson and Dick Campbell have indelibly left their fingerprints on me. Although they are dead now, I remained as close as possible to them until their last days. I was a surrogate son for both; neither had any children of their own and looked with a degree of paternal pride on everything that I did. They made a great difference in my life.

CARL COX © 1998

Elizabeth Dole

As the former president of the American Red Cross, the world's foremost humanitarian organization, Elizabeth Dole oversaw more than 30,700 paid employees and 1.3 million volunteers. Under her leadership, the American Red Cross was consistently recognized for its outstanding financial stewardship. Mrs. Dole has continued a remarkable public service career in which she has served five U.S. presidents and has been named by the Gallup poll as one of the world's most admired women.

A native of Salisbury, North Carolina, Elizabeth Dole earned a degree from Harvard Law School in 1965 and also holds a master's degree in education and government from Harvard University. In February 1983, she joined President Ronald Reagan's cabinet as secretary of transportation—the first woman to hold that position, and in 1989 she was sworn in by President George Bush as the nation's twentieth secretary of labor.

WHEN I WAS A CHILD, life offered far fewer choices for females. Yet in my small hometown of Salisbury, North Carolina, I looked to a horizon without limits, thanks to a wonderful society of nurturing women. They guided, encouraged, inspired, and—perhaps the greatest gift one can give a child—they believed in me. From my earliest years, my mother, Mary Hanford, created the loving environment that freed me to explore an ever-widening world. My grandmother, Mom Cathey, showed me a vital, joyous religious faith that remains my life's greatest blessing.

Beyond my family, I found remarkable role models in my teachers. One of the most gifted was Mrs. W. W. Weant. Sixth-grade civics leaped to life when she led class trips and then had us report our findings to other classes. She kindled lively discussions on current events that brought the world into our classroom. She encouraged my love of books, awakened my interest in public speaking, and nurtured personal relationships with each of us by visiting our homes and engaging our parents in our school lives.

Like all great teachers, she ignited in her students a love of learning. In my admiration for her, I stretched to do more: to start my own little library and book club, to clip articles that supplemented our class studies, to labor in the remedial workbooks she gave me in order to overcome my weak arithmetic. At the time I was doing it for her, but wise Mrs. Weant knew I was the ultimate beneficiary.

When I entered Duke University, I once again benefited from the guidance of an exceptional woman. Dean Florence Brinkley was a tall, stately woman who taught her students to think for themselves. After I was elected student government president, we worked closely on many initiatives, including the establishment of a leadership training program for women.

After graduating from Duke and earning a master's degree, I sought an audience with Margaret Chase Smith, a feisty independent Maine Republican regarded by many as the conscience of the U.S. Senate. How many busy legislators would share an hour with a total stranger? In her brisk and efficient way, Senator Smith welcomed me into her private office and offered her counsel: I should bolster my education with a law degree so that I could bring more to a public policy job than aptitude and enthusiasm. I took her advice and vowed to repay my debt to her by keeping my own door open to young women seeking advice.

The pattern has repeated itself throughout my career: women who had gained a foothold on the executive ladder reached down a hand to me. On the updraft of such women, I've been privileged to soar.

HUGH DOWNS

MIA DRAKE BRANDT

Hugh Downs, one of the most familiar American television figures in the history of the medium, is the coanchor of ABC New's *20/20*, the prime-time weekly newsmagazine. He has enjoyed a distinguished career in radio and television as a reporter, newscaster, interviewer, narrator, and host. In May 1989 he celebrated his fiftieth anniversary in broadcasting—both on radio and television. In July 1957 he helped launch *The Tonight Show* with Jack Paar and stayed with the late-night series for five years. From 1962 to 1971, Downs was also host of the NBC News's *Today* program.

Mr. Downs is chairman of the board of governors of the National Space Society, chairman of the board of the United States Committee for UNICEF, a trustee of the Menninger Foundation, and has served as a member of the National Aeronautics and Space Administration (NASA) Advisory Council.

My first inspiration was found within a list. In 1944, St. John's College of Maryland published a list of 131 classic tomes of the Western world. I was in my twenties at the time and mapped out a seven-year plan to read them. It took me thirteen years to complete the adventure. I started when I was twenty-two, and there are still books on the list that I continue to reread. My mother read me *Huckleberry Finn* when I was a child; I read it again in my twenties and reread it again in my fifties. My view of the book has changed as my worldview has matured. That's the greatest aspect of reading: books seem to grow with you.

When I hosted *Live From Lincoln Center* I came into contact with some of the world's greatest living musical artists. The range of personalities was immense. There were musicians like the pianist Andre Watts, who was remarkable under tremendous pressure. But you would never know it from his preshow demeanor. He would talk with you right up until the time he was to perform and would almost have to be dragged from his conversation to the stage. At the opposite end of the spectrum was a soprano prima donna (whom I will not name) who was very critical and harsh with people but was an amazing performer. But if you divert your energy with these types of antics, how is that going to translate into the rest of your life? Professionally it may work—you may still get the job done—but personally you are going to be a mess.

I was inspired by most of the musicians with whom I came in contact. Yo Yo Ma and Pablo Casals, two of the greatest cello players, are good examples of individuals secure in their artistry who do not need to bolster their position with dramatics.

I once profiled Dr. Stephen J. Hawking and got a glimpse into that brilliant cauldron of his mind. I had studied theoretical physics since I was fifteen, when my brother first got me interested in the subject. Supposedly, twelve people in the world understood general relativity, and my brother and I wanted to be the thirteenth and fourteenth.

I spent four evenings with Dr. Hawking at his home, and he examined my own theory of missing mass in the universe. Of course, he found a flaw in my theory that I had overlooked. Over the course of those evenings I discovered that he thought special relativity, a concept that supposedly anyone can grasp, was more difficult to explain than general relativity. I wondered if his grasp of quantum mechanics helped him in this. He told me that he understood general relativity before he even heard of quantum mechanics, which means that when he was a young man he had read Einstein's theory and instantly understood it. He is truly an incredible individual.

He told me that he wouldn't choose to be in his condition—he suffers from Lou Gehrig's Disease—but that he continues to be driven in his questioning of the structure and function of the universe. He is very much an optimist and said that he almost viewed his condition as a positive aspect of his life. It is a way, he said, that he can be excused from social obligations and spend all his time thinking about the questions that he has devoted his life to.

Doctors diagnose people in his condition as living with the disease seven or eight years at the most. Stephen Hawking has made it thirty years past the expectancy the doctors predicted for him. He keeps himself going through some immense power of will. He is, I think, a very strong example of the power of mind over matter.

Dr. Hawking reminds me of the Stoic philosophy found within the *Meditations* of Marcus Aurelius, one of the books on the St. John's list. The philosophy says that you should start with humble steps and be concerned with only that which is in your power. If you apply this maxim to Stephen Hawking, you realize how much is possible within the confines of what is termed a limitation.

CHILDREN'S DEFENSE FUND

Marian Wright Edelman

Marian Wright Edelman, founder and president of the Children's Defense Fund (CDF), has been an advocate for disadvantaged Americans her entire career. Under her leadership, the Washington-based CDF has become a strong national voice for children and families.

Mrs. Edelman, a graduate of Spelman College and Yale Law School, began her career in the mid-1960s, when, as the first black woman admitted to the Mississippi bar, she directed the NAACP Legal Defense and Educational Fund office in Jackson, Mississippi. In 1968, she moved to Washington, D.C., as counsel for the Poor People's March that Dr. Martin Luther King Jr. began organizing before his death. She also founded the Washington Research Project, a public-interest law firm and the parent body of the Children's Defense Fund and for two years served as the director of the Center for Law and Education at Harvard University. In 1973 she began the CDF.

I GREW UP IN BENNETTSVILLE, SOUTH CAROLINA, the daughter of a Baptist preacher. My parents had the most important influence on me while I was growing up and are responsible for the values I received as a child. I also fell under the influence of the community elders, who saw themselves as an essential part in the raising of the town's children. It was a role that was expected of them.

I went to Spelman College in Atlanta. It was a staid woman's college that developed safe, young women who married Morehouse men, helped raise a family, and never kicked up dust.

My history professor there, Howard Zinn, taught me the value of questioning the status quo and illustrated the power inherent in an individual. Professor Zinn got us involved in the political climate of the times. This was the South of the late 1950s, where the first attempts at social and political change in the struggle for civil rights originated.

Professor Zinn would take us outside the sheltered stone wall of the Spelman gates to the realities of interracial dialogues and protests. The activism we initially took part in preceded the regional and national movements that are usually referred to as the civil rights era. One of our first actions was to protest the policy of public library segregation. Protesters (predominately college students) walked into the Carnegie Library in Atlanta asking librarians for such works as John Stuart Mill's *On Liberty* or John Locke's *An Essay Concerning Human Understanding*. Some asked for the U.S. Constitution and others for the Declaration of Independence. Using such tactics, the Atlanta Library Board changed its segregationist policy. It was actions such as these that led to further protests, further questioning, and striving for basic American freedoms. It was the beginning of a movement for many of us.

Professor Zinn was instrumental in helping me get a fellowship for a junior year abroad. He had a lot of faith in me as a young girl and felt that traveling on my own would benefit me more than going with the Smith or Sweetbriar groups.

I left the United States in 1958 and traveled through Europe for fifteen months. My year abroad gave me the confidence to take risks and follow my own path. It made me more of an individual; it gave me a sense of myself. It also exposed me to the possibilities of the world. There was so much out there, so much to see and experience. My year abroad was a very special time; it was a time of awakening.

I returned to Atlanta to find a more socially and racially tense city. Opinions had grown stronger on both sides, and the consequences of those opinions were taking shape in the worst of ways. Professor Zinn continued to involve students in civil rights issues and led them to more protests and rallies.

It was also at this time that I decided to go to law school. It was something I had never thought of before, but somewhere in the course of my travels it became a reality for me. I graduated from Spelman in 1960 and went to Yale Law School. After receiving my degree I returned to Mississippi to continue my activism with the Student Nonviolent Coordinating Committee, which organized most of the voter registrations and protests for blacks in the Deep South, many resulting in violent confrontations with small-town law officers and locals.

Professor Zinn responded to a yearning in the younger generation to make a difference, and like all good teachers, he brought out the best in people. He was concerned with justice, and everyone around him caught his concern. He was a very special man whose political activities eventually got him fired from Spelman. He went on to Boston University and became an outspoken critic of the Vietnam War.

Well into his seventies, Professor Zinn remains an optimist. He has been a prolific writer of numerous books, including the controversial *A People's History of the United States* and *You Can't Be Neutral on a Moving Train*. He doesn't teach anymore, but is a very busy public speaker. I am grateful to him for fostering in me the belief that I could make a difference; it is something I have carried with me ever since.

As I watched Andrew Young being sworn in as the mayor of Atlanta in 1981, I felt such a sense of accomplishment. Before the ceremony, I ate lunch in a cafeteria where I had protested and been arrested years before. I had come full circle.

GLORIA ESTEFAN

MATHEW ROLSTON

Since bursting into the public eye in 1985 as the enigmatic front woman of Miami Sound Machine, Gloria Estefan has been in a state of perpetual, often radical, creative evolution. "There's not growth without a lot of hard work and a little risk," she says. "It's important to me that I continue to grow. There's no point in living any other way."

As she segued into a solo recording career—with Miami Sound Machine members continuing to contribute—Gloria became the only Latin artist to achieve major mainstream worldwide success.

In 1975, she met her husband and producer-songwriter Emilio Estefan Jr. at a wedding where Emilio and his band were performing. He coaxed her into singing two songs and then offered her a job. Three years later the two had formed a deep romantic bond in addition to an unbreakable musical connection.

THERE IS ONLY ONE PERSON IN MY LIFE whom I consider my mentor—my grandmother on my mother's side, Consuelo Garcia. Besides her obvious role as a grandparent, she represented to me a vivid example of a woman ahead of her time. She was a strong, caring, spiritual humanitarian who filled my life with possibilities and through her example gave me the belief that there was nothing I could not do or achieve in life. Although she was born in 1905 in Cuba, she felt no limitations and even aspired to be a lawyer, an unheard of profession for a Latin woman. And though she had to leave school to help her large family at the age of ten, she taught herself to read and write and became an amazingly astute businesswoman and extremely independent.

She cared for me from birth and nurtured the thought that music was a gift I had received. And although I was reluctant to follow that path, I somehow found myself involved with music because our gifts are meant to be shared for the good and pleasure of others. We remained extremely close throughout my life, and even after her death I have often found comfort in her memory and the wisdom she shared with me.

It is difficult to pick one specific meaningful experience that we shared because there were many unusual and uncanny experiences that became commonplace as our lives intertwined more and more. We shared a unique psychic connection, and it became impossible for me to go through difficult situations without my grandmother somehow "knowing." She was very aware of and quite comfortable with this unusual gift and became instrumental in my discovery of my own intuitiveness as well. It is something I have drawn upon in many instances in life.

My grandmother always pointed out my strengths and filled me with hope for the future. She constantly nourished my inquisitiveness and shared many quests for seeking answers to my questions. She wasn't afraid to let me see her vulnerability, and made that intimacy an asset to be celebrated. Primarily through her example I learned that we, as women, have limitless potential. I finally said yes to music because of her.

Singing "came with me" into this life, but I was not pursuing it as a career. I studied psychology, communications, and languages, but she repeatedly told me that I would be happiest doing something I loved. Often she would bring people in the music business to listen to me, and somehow with gentle prodding try to sway me. But she knew that it would have to be me that chose a musical career. I'm happy to have followed her advice because she was right. I finally chose the best career for myself.

The turning point in my life came when I auditioned for my band, Miami Latin Boys, which would later become Miami Sound Machine. I took my mother, sister, and grandmother to the audition. I initially joined the band as a hobby, but my grandmother told me after I had been accepted that I had probably taken the most important step of my life.

The most valuable lessons I learned from my grandmother were to discover what makes you happy and *do it* with as much energy and joy as you can muster. And that success takes perseverance, determination, and an unwavering belief in what you have chosen to do.

I feel fortunate to have found such an amazing mentor. I don't believe that people like my grandmother are commonplace, or even a given within a family. She had a profound influence on who I am and continues to be my inspiration.

GIRLS SCOUTS OF U.S.A.

Elinor J. Ferdon

Elinor J. Ferdon is the national president of Girl Scouts of the U.S.A. She was elected to the office, the highest volunteer position in girl scouting, in October 1996.

Mrs. Ferdon has served in various capacities in girl scouting for more than thirty years, and proudly describes herself as a "volunteer professional." She has been on the Girl Scout National Board of Directors since 1978, most recently serving as first vice president and executive committee chair. Her volunteer activities outside of girl scouting are extensive as well. She sits on the United Way of America Board of Governors and is vice chair of the board of trustees of Liberty Science Center.

Mrs. Ferdon has also been involved in girl scouting internationally. She served five years as president of the World Foundation for Girl Guides and Girl Scouts, Inc.

Her honors include the Thanks Badge and Thanks Badge Two, girl scouting's highest recognition for adults, and an honorary doctorate from Fairleigh Dickinson University.

TO PARAPHRASE A FORMER governor of New Jersey: "Mentoring and leadership—made for each other!" The women and men who influenced my life were extraordinary. And because of them I am the national president of Girl Scouts of the U.S.A., serving as a leader, role model, and mentor for millions of girls and young women.

My father was an officer in the U.S. Army, and our family moved constantly. Because it seemed important that I begin to develop "roots" in one community, I spent a great deal of time with my grandparents in Stonington, Connecticut. My grandfather, Stuart Weston Webb, a former president of a Boston bank during the stock market crash of 1929, served as my first inspirational figure because he always pushed the boundaries of my life. While others told me that I could become a wonderful homemaker, nurse, or secretary, he would tell me what a great leader I could be. He always motivated me to strive for something greater. He told me to "be all I could be" before the phrase became a popular slogan. As a result, I realized there were many opportunities for girls and women. He really opened my eyes at a fairly young age.

When I was fifteen, I enrolled in the Mary A. Burnham School for Girls in Northampton, Massachusetts. It was an all-girl environment that offered a strong support network of peers and teachers. It was also a place to test scholastic and social ideas. The headmistress of the school was Miriam Peters, who was very supportive and pushed me to work harder in all aspects of my school life. At one point my grades for the quarter were not as good as they had been, and as she expected of me. She took me into her office and said I had better things to do with my brain than to waste it. She told me that I had great leadership potential and that I needed to stay at the top of my class to achieve that potential. She said, "You have the brains and you can do it." I applied myself harder to my studies because I admired, trusted, and did not want to disappoint her.

My English teacher at Mary A. Burnham, Dr. Mildred Prince, recognized the importance of building girls' self-esteem. She did this by encouraging us to be good public speakers and emphasizing the importance of speech design and its delivery. She helped me learn that the "butterflies" I acquired before each speech were okay. And, she chose me to read the daily announcements at the morning chapel gatherings of the student body. Through this I gained the self-confidence needed to excel at public speaking. Ninety-five percent of what I do now is give speeches to groups of hundreds or more. I am thankful to have had this ability nurtured in me at a young age.

A great love of mine in my youth, and today, is sports. In school I loved team sports, and was pretty good too. Our coaches, who were clearly acting as mentors, saw this and strove to develop my leadership skills on the athletic field. I was encouraged to be the captain of several teams, which served me well when I became an adult. To be a successful leader on or off the athletic field, one must know the individuals who come together as a team to make a whole; teamwork *is* about many becoming one. Excelling in sports helped me become aware of the importance of my teammates and was another way in which my self-esteem was developed. I learned a lot serving as a team captain.

The women and men who were my mentors during my youth, encouraging me every step of the way, had an exceptional impact on me. The values formed in my personal life are a direct result of these experiences. Now I can be the adult who widens a child's boundaries; I can try to inspire girls to develop the skills within them, to "be all they can be." I have come full circle.

As national president of Girl Scouts of the U.S.A., I take my responsibility to serve as a role model for 3.5 million Girl Scouts seriously. It is my hope that they, too, will become mentors and influence and serve as role models for millions more girls and young women of the twenty-first century. If I can influence or inspire others in the manner in which I was inspired to become a community leader, I will have accomplished what those who cared about me dreamed I would become.

It has been said that the future is not a gift, it is achieved. Through the efforts of individual mentors, young people can dream of a future in which they will be important in all aspects of society and become successful at everything they attempt.

Geraldine Ferraro

Geraldine Ferraro has earned a place in history as the first woman vice-presidential candidate on a national party ticket. In 1978 she was first elected to Congress from New York's Ninth Congressional District, in Queens, New York, and served three terms in the House of Representatives. In Congress, Ferraro spearheaded efforts to achieve passage of the Equal Rights Amendment. She also sponsored the Woman's Economic Equity Act, which ended pension discrimination against women, provided job options for displaced homemakers, and enabled homemakers to open individual retirement accounts (IRAs).

In 1994, she was appointed the U.S. ambassador to the United Nations Human Rights Commission by President Bill Clinton and served in that position through 1996. From 1996 to 1998, Ms. Ferraro was a cohost of *Crossfire*, a political interview program, on CNN. An active participant in the nation's foreign policy debate, she serves as a board member of the National Democratic Institute of International Affairs and is a member of the Council on Foreign Relations.

MY MOTHER, ANTONETTA, taught me how to live life. She had experienced many setbacks in her own life yet never let them get the best of her. She lost one child when he was six days old. Another son was killed in an automobile accident when he was three. My father died when my mother was thirty-nine, and some difficult financial times followed as she worked to raise my brother and me. But she never complained, and whenever I suffered a setback she would say, "Deal with the situation, learn from your mistakes, and move on." She was a strong woman who lived a tough life, but she remained an optimist throughout. It was probably that optimism and her devotion to her children that kept her going.

My mother also believed quite strongly that I could become whatever I wanted to be. This was rather unusual for the time and for her culture. Most Italian Americans did not feel that women had options in life. The prevailing notion of the time was that a woman's place was in the home, raising a family. My mother considered that a laudable life choice but only one of many. She saw no reason that a woman's potential should be limited simply because she was born female. She was obviously ahead of her time.

My mother's unwavering belief in me and my ability was the main reason I was able to succeed. I saw possibilities in everything. Fueled by her encouragement, I launched myself into my studies and found joy in academics. Perhaps because she had to go to work to support younger brothers and sisters when she was thirteen, my mother directed her energies to making certain both my brother and I would have the education that she had been denied. Her work as a crochet beader, hunched over a wooden frame for hours on end, gave me the tools to win scholarships. Her encouragement got me through law school at night. My mother remained the main influence in my life until her death, but when I entered Congress I also acquired a political mentor.

In 1978, I won a seat in the House of Representatives. It was then that I met "Tip" O'Neill. He was not only the Speaker, he was a father figure, a great teacher, and a superb politician. Having lost my own father at a young age, it meant a great deal to me that he would spend time with me. In 1984, Tip was the first person to suggest my name as the Democratic nominee for vice president.

My mother died in 1990, but she left me a blueprint for life that I continue to follow. She stressed that I have been blessed by good things in life and that I have an obligation to pay back. She also cautioned that I should never forget where I came from. I've always attempted to do just that. For her.

LAURENCE FISHBURNE

Laurence Fishburne has been acting in films and onstage since he was ten, starting in the soap opera *One Life to Live,* then making his feature film debut in *Cornbread, Earl and Me,* at twelve. At fifteen, he was heading off to the Philippines to work for the epic motion picture *Apocalypse Now.* In 1992, he was awarded a Tony, a Drama Desk Award, an Outer Critic's Circle Award, and a Theater World Award for his role as Sterling Johnson in August Wilson's *Two Trains Running.* His rare television appearance in the 1993 premiere episode of Fox TV's *Tribeca* landed him an Emmy, and he was nominated for an Oscar for his portrayal of Ike Turner in the film *What's Love Got to Do With It.* His versatility is a gift, and he has been able to land roles not initially earmarked for black actors.

I HAVE HAD THE GOOD FORTUNE to have the influence of many mentors in my life. Aside from my parents, Maurice Watson was my first mentor. He is an educator of the highest order. His influence on my life has been immeasurable because he showered unconditional love upon me. He has been consistently caring in my personal life and in regards to my career, from my youth right up to the present day.

When I was sixteen, I remember listening to Francis Coppola and cinematographer Vittorio Sorarro discussing filmmaking. This was a turning point of my life, for I was able to understand their passion and realize that I, too, could pursue an artistic life.

As a playwright, I now look to August Wilson for inspiration. After hearing my acceptance speech at the Tony Awards in 1992, he said to me, "I'm gonna get you a pen and some paper, 'cause you need to be writing."

My friendship with Roscoe Lee Brown is one of the great joys of my life. His gentleness, wisdom, and intelligence inspire me every day that I live—in my humble attempts to emulate his manner, his way of speaking, his way of simply being. I find that my sense of self is much improved. It was Roscoe Lee Brown who influenced me to use my given name professionally.

The most valuable lessons I learned from my mentors are these: one, always remain openhearted and open-minded; and two, you get more flies with honey than with vinegar.

WHOOPI GOLDBERG

Whoopi Goldberg began performing at the age of eight in New York. Later she moved to Berkeley, where she did stand-up comedy. *The Color Purple* launched her film career, earning her an Oscar nomination, a 1985 Golden Globe Award, and an NAACP Image Award. Her performance in *Ghost* earned her an Academy Award, a Golden Globe, and another NAACP Image Award. She was also honored by Harvard University's Hasty Pudding Theatricals as its 1993 Woman of the Year.

Whoopi has extensive television experience. Her appearances on *Moonlighting* and *A Different World* earned her Prime-Time Emmy Award nominations. Rodgers and Hammerstein's *Cinderella* earned her another Image Award nomination. She hosted the Grammy Awards in 1992, and the Academy Awards in 1994 and 1996.

Whoopi is well-known for her humanitarian efforts on behalf of children, the homeless, human rights, substance abuse, and AIDS, as well as many other causes and charities.

In 1995, she fulfilled a childhood fantasy by becoming part of Hollywood history when she placed prints of her hands, feet, and braids in cement in the forecourt of Mann's Chinese Theatre.

MY MOTHER, EMMA, is a great, great person. She had all the right ingredients that influenced me as I was growing up. She was a chaperone when we were taking a school field trip once. It was at a time when everyone was starting to form cliques. I wanted to be in a clique so badly. I wanted to be in a cool group. At the time of the field trip, I had just gotten in one of these groups and was very happy. However, everyone in the car was making fun of a friend of mine, but I wasn't doing anything about it. In fact, I was taking part. My mother, who was driving, stayed quiet the entire time.

After the trip, my mom noted that this friend had had a really tough day with all the kids in the car giving him such a rough time, and she was surprised that I didn't do something to help him. "I know how you hate it when people make fun of you or when people hurt your feelings. I'm surprised that you would hurt someone else's." It was like someone had hit me over the head with a baseball bat. It was a fundamental lesson that I have kept with me as years have passed and things have gotten more complex: treat people like you want to be treated and always meet people and interact with them on an individual basis.

I was also fortunate enough to have gone to a summer camp, Madison Felica, for a number of years in Peekskill, New York. The camp was an extraordinary experience for me. I met people from all walks of life, many of whom remain good friends. It seems that I came into contact with the right people at the right time.

I look back at those times and those friends and see how I got to be the way I am today. I'm a composite of so many people that I have known. It's like I was a sponge absorbing them. Those friends really helped to shape me. They also offered an outlet for things going on in my life. I could share the best and the worst with them and know that they would be there for me. And I tried to be there for them as well.

Over the years, so many people have set me on this path and taught me so much. One of the most important lessons I have learned is that, as an individual, you have the capacity to achieve a goal. You have to apply yourself, and by applying, learn the ritual of trying. You may not accomplish your goal, but the idea is trying to get there. Belief in progress and moving forward is very important. Even if you don't attain your goal, you should at least realize that you have tried, and that in attempting you have achieved a great deal. Failure is not an end in itself. It is simply a means of continuing forward.

I learned this lesson from my mom and my friends. I'm very grateful to them for helping me to learn this.

OFFICIAL WHITE HOUSE PHOTO

Tipper Gore

Tipper Gore is a well-known advocate for families, women, and children, and is actively involved in issues related to mental health, education, and homelessness. As mental health policy adviser to the president, she is committed to eradicating the stigma of mental illness and educating Americans about the need for quality, affordable mental health care. She also serves as special adviser to the Interagency Council on the Homeless and cochair of the Department of Education's initiative, America Goes Back to School.

Mrs. Gore grew up in Arlington, Virginia. She received a B.A. in psychology from Boston University, and a master's degree in psychology from George Peabody College at Vanderbilt University in 1975. She worked as a newspaper photographer for the *Nashville Tennessean* until her husband was elected to Congress in 1976. In 1996, Mrs. Gore published

Picture This, A Visual Diary, which is a personal photographic representation of life as wife of Vice President Al Gore.

I HAVE ALWAYS FELT that it is important to revere and honor older people for their experience and wisdom. Perhaps that feeling grew from the meaningful role that my grandparents played in my upbringing. I remember most vividly my grandmother's influence and wisdom. She told countless stories about her family and upbringing. Through the telling of these stories, she taught many lessons and provided a sense of continuity to the past as we shared time in the present. She taught me her skills: cooking, sewing, gardening, and managing relationships. Whenever I had a problem I would go to her with it and she would help me sort through the different issues. Sometimes she would just issue the solution, which was comforting in itself. I felt that she was always there for me, right or wrong, to listen and to love me.

I was raised in a religious household where personal morality mattered a lot. My grandmother helped instill in me a very strong sense of right and wrong and personal responsibility. She always told me, "Don't neglect your education. It's the one thing nobody can take from you."

Outside my family, one of my strongest lifelong interests has been the art of photography, an interest that grew from the encouragement of another mentor in my life. When my husband and I lived on a small farm fifty miles from Nashville, Jack Corn was the photo editor for the *Tennessean,* the local newspaper in Nashville. My husband had given me a camera and I began taking a photography class with Jack, driving one hundred miles round-trip to attend each session. He taught me everything, from the principles of photojournalism to printing and processing pictures. He gave me tremendous encouragement. Even more than that, he offered me a part-time job at the *Tennessean.*

I started out in the photo lab, developing film, and progressed to printing pictures, and finally to shooting them. After a while I began doing photo essays, taking the pictures and writing the text. When the paper published them, it convinced me that I could make a contribution outside the home and family, and that photography was a means to communicate about larger social issues. When the paper published my photograph of an evicted woman sitting on a curb in the rain, I was gratified. But when calls to help her flooded the newspaper, I realized the power of the photograph to communicate a human being's personal pain, and that power could move people to help their fellow man.

While Jack saw photography as art, he primarily viewed it as a form of communication. Today, my love of photography, nurtured through the interest that Jack took in my work, lets me capture images of my family as well as some truly historic moments that have taken place during my husband's term as vice president of the United States.

STEPHEN JAY GOULD

RHONDA ROLAND SHEARER

Dr. Stephen Jay Gould is one of the world's best-known scientists and has been a bestselling author for more than a decade. Coauthor of the groundbreaking evolutionary theory of punctuated equilibrium, Gould is a leading advocate for science education and the premier interpreter of Darwinian theory. His most recent book is *Rock of Ages: Science and Religion in the Fullness of Life,* an insightful, brief history of the false conflict between science and religion throughout the ages. Author of the longest running series of contemporary essays, which have appeared monthly in *National History* since January 1974, Dr. Gould is the Alexander Agassiz professor of zoology and a professor of geology at Harvard University. He also serves as the Vincent Astor visiting professor of biology at New York University. He lives in Cambridge, Massachusetts, and New York City.

THE FIRST MAJOR INFLUENCE of my life was seeing the skeleton of a Tyrannosaurus rex in the American Museum of Natural History. There were only two in the world at the time—in the New York and Pittsburgh museums—and this gigantic skeleton fired my imagination. Rural kids find fossils. Urban kids go to museums. I was glad I was an urban kid.

People say career paths are sometimes chosen at an early age. For me, I wanted to deal with fossils. A colleague, Al Romer, a former director of the museum, told me this story. When he was a kid in upstate New York, he was bitten by a dog and had to go to New York City for two weeks to get all the proper shots. When he wasn't at the hospital, he went to the museum. It turned out that he was inspired by the same skeleton I was—and this was about fifty years before I saw it!

I also had a fifth-grade teacher, Esther Ponti, at P.S. 26 in Queens, who played a huge part in my choice of science as a career. What set her apart from the others was her respect for children. She really strove to foster children's interests and creativity. In our particular class, she recognized that a number of us were interested in science. Although she didn't particularly know much about science, she wanted to make it more available to those who showed an interest in it. So she gathered our scientific-minded fifth graders and set aside time for us once a week to meet in the back of the classroom to hold our "self-help" science club. She would bring in science books that people recommended to her and just let us go. I stayed in correspondence with her for more than thirty years, until she died.

You can't stop real self-starters. They don't need to be pushed, they just need not be suppressed. However, parents and teachers can unwittingly do just that. Think how many people will not sing because some teacher once told them when they were young to mouth the words of the national anthem because they were singing off-key. That's unfair to children. What affects them at a young age can stick with them for life. You have to encourage them. It can make such a difference in their lives.

Richard Grasso

USED WITH THE PERMISSION OF THE NYSE

Richard A. Grasso has been chairman and CEO of the New York Stock Exchange since June 1995. He is the first member of the NYSE to be elected to these positions in the exchange's 206-year history.

Mr. Grasso has assigned the highest priorities to assuring the NYSE's position as a premier global equities market, enhancing its competitive edge by applying cutting-edge technology to trading, regulation, and administration; and upholding the NYSE's bedrock corporate values, which include integrity, excellence, respect for the individual, and a customer-comes-first orientation.

Mr. Grasso is also chairman of the YMCA of greater New York and a member of the boards of the Centurion Foundation, the New York City Police Foundation, New

York City Public Private Initiatives, Inc., the National Italian-American Foundation, the Tinker Foundation, and the Yale School of Management. He cochairs Project Smart Schools, a program designed to provide computers for New York City classrooms and computer-related training for teachers.

I GREW UP IN QUEENS and started working a series of odd jobs when I was about 10 or 11, the first of which was for Moe, the owner of a local candy store.

Moe was a big, burly guy who embodied hard work and the local color of the community. He was a typical small business owner—his store was open seven days a week with shorter hours on Sundays, and also served as a community center to catch up on the local news. My coworkers and I, all kids, would put newspapers together in the back of the store. As I did this I would listen to the conversations between Moe and his customers, learning a lot about my community, as Moe and his friends would catch up on gossip and current events. It was a little bit of income, but a lot of education.

Then, as a teenager, I started working for Harry Rosenbaum, the owner of a local pharmacy. Although he was a pharmacist by vocation, he was an investor by avocation—a small business owner interested in big business. He provided my first introduction to the stock market, which taught me a lot, mostly because of his keen interest and informative following of the market.

In 1974, I started working for John Phelan. He had followed in the footsteps of his father and initially worked for his father's market-making business on the trading floor of the New York Stock Exchange. However, in 1975, John became vice chairman of the NYSE and left his father's business in a working capacity. Later, in 1980, he severed all ties with his father's firm in order to become president of the NYSE and part of the exchange's senior management.

John taught me about life and the intricacies of the market. He was a visionary who valued a person's ability above and beyond their color or creed. I would say that he is responsible for where I am today and for the current success of the NYSE. I know I would not be the same, personally or professionally, without having worked with him. He is sixty-seven now and remains very active in the professional world. We still get together for dinners to talk. He is still a friend and a mentor, and it is an honor to know him.

ANTONIO MAURI

Lorraine E. Hale

Dr. Lorraine E. Hale has been at the forefront of infant care in America for twenty-five years. With her mother, the legendary Clara "Mother" Hale, she cofounded the famed Hale House in 1969.

On an April day in 1969, after leaving her mother's apartment, Dr. Hale sat in her car waiting for a light to change. She eyed a woman with a baby sitting on a box by the curb, and recognized her as a drug addict. Dr. Hale left her car, approached the woman, and asked if she needed help. Dr. Hale explained that her mother took care of babies and would gladly keep hers. Within six months, Mother Hale's apartment had twenty-two babies, all born of drug-abusing mothers. At the encouragement of a friend, Lorraine E. Hale wrote and submitted a proposal to the Office of Economic Opportunity. The proposal was funded and Hale House was born. Mother Hale passed away in 1992 and Dr. Lorraine E. Hale has continued the legacy and tradition of loving, infant care to a generation of children who would have been forgotten.

ONE OF MY JUNIOR HIGH school teachers at P.S. 81 in Harlem had a profound influence on my life. I was in an advanced-education class, which meant that I would complete three years of education in two. I was a pretty good student, but I talked all the time. My teacher, Mrs. Kane, took me aside one day and told me something that I will never forget. She said that I was the only person she had ever met who didn't want to be smart. "Lorraine, don't you know how smart you are? Don't you know how smart, bright, and pretty you are?" I was stunned. No one had ever said that to me before. Inside, I always wanted it to be true but no one had ever told me that outloud.

Almost immediately, my behavior in class and my attitude toward just about everything changed. I became more interested in school and started taking part in class discussions, because I *did* want to be smart. Well, I knew I was already smart—I was ready to be smarter!

I immersed myself in books. I read all the time. It is a passion that I still have today. I've always felt that books held the answers. I didn't necessarily believe my teachers, but I would believe my books, because they spoke to me in ways that people never really could. They opened up entire worlds to me, worlds that somehow belonged to me. It was uncanny how a book I was reading at the time invariably related to my life somehow.

As a child I read all the classics. I might not have understood the entire message the author was trying to convey, but I did grasp a lot anyway. I remember reading *Moby-Dick.* I must have been about eleven or twelve at the time. There was just something about it, an anger there that I understood. The whale was angry because he had been attacked. He was just trying to say, "Don't do that." I could understand the whale's anger because I saw the same anger in Harlem growing up. People were always nice there but I saw a core of anger in some folks. Even as a child, I could relate to it. Like the whale, these people were saying, "Don't do that. Don't do that."

My father died when I was young. After his death, my family had little money and sometimes none. One day I was walking to the store when a lady stopped me on the street and told me that I was too big to have safety pins in my clothes. She said it so kindly and compassionately that I wasn't insulted or embarrassed. She asked if I felt comfortable walking with her somewhere. When I answered no, she asked me to wait for her and walked off into a store. Returning minutes later, she handed me a small box. Inside were several spools of thread, buttons, and a couple of sewing needles. "You are too big to have safety pins in your clothes," she repeated, and she walked off. But her action and her compassion spoke to me. I count it as a turning point in my life.

There is no mistaking the power of positive feedback in a child's life. As adults, we need to always take the opportunity to let children know how important and precious they are. It takes so little to motivate them. Just a few gentle words can have a lasting positive effect. It was the case with me, and I've seen it work with so many.

At Hale House we pay special attention to our children, who need to be dealt with gently. When the children come to us they have no family, so as we become their family it's important to give them a sense of their own worth, potential, and independence. Hopefully, the lessons I learned from those who took time out for me are being passed on to a new generation. And someday, I hope that each of the children here at Hale House will make a difference in another child's life. That's how it should be.

Pete Hamill

FRED R. CONRAD/NEW YORK TIMES

Pete Hamill is a novelist, journalist, editor, and screenwriter. For four decades, his journalism has appeared in almost all major American magazines. He has served as editor in chief of the *New York Post* and the *New York Daily News.* He is the winner of numerous awards, including the Meyer Berger Award and the Twenty-Five-Year-Achievement award of the Silurians Society.

His writing has not been limited to journalism. Hamill has published eight novels, two short story collections, two journalism anthologies, and the bestselling memoir *A Drinking Life.* His essay on the future of newspapers, *News Is a Verb,* is currently in bookstores. His latest book, *Why Sinatra Matters,* is an extended essay on the music and life of the late singer.

As a journalist, he covered wars in Vietnam, Northern Ireland, Lebanon, and Nicaragua; the fall of communism in

Czechoslovakia; political conventions, the World Series, the riots of the 1960s, assorted murders, championship fights, and an occasional three-alarm fire.

OUTSIDE MY FAMILY, there were no mentors in any conventional sense. I did have one huge role model (although that awful phrase was thankfully not in use): Jackie Robinson. His example was there for all of us. He was intense, passionate, focused. He always pushed his talent to its furthest limit. In 1947, the year he became the first black American to play in the major leagues, he was the epitome of stoic values. No matter how brutal the outside pressure might be (from racists and the media), he kept his mouth shut and played ball. If he could do that, in the face of such terrible provocation, we could too. It's a half century later, the Brooklyn Dodgers are gone, and so is Jackie Robinson. But I still find myself asking, in time of personal or professional difficulty: How would Jackie handle this?

Where I grew up in Brooklyn, nobody had ever gone to college, and few had even finished high school. But while serving in the U.S. Navy, a number of people encouraged me to go on to get a general equivalency degree (GED), and use the GI Bill as a means of attending college. I did. At Pratt Institute, a marvelous teacher named Tom McMahon encouraged me to write. He organized a small group of us—all comrades from Brooklyn—into a reading group, and every week we focused intensely on certain classics. We read Hemingway, Fitzgerald. We spent many weeks analyzing Aristotle's *Ethics.* I'm sure that McMahon realized that we would have to understand issues of right and wrong before we could do anything with our lives. Until it was destroyed a few years ago in a fire, I carried my copy of the Penguin paperback edition of the *Ethics* with me for more than forty years. It was at once a study of moral philosophy and an artifact of my youth. Once in a while, I would open it and smile at the young man who had studied it so intently; he had underlined all the wrong passages.

I became a newspaperman in 1960, working nights at the old *New York Post*. I was untrained, immensely ignorant of the craft. But some master craftsmen guided me along the way. Ed Kosner, later editor of *Newsweek, Esquire,* and *New York* magazine, helped me through some of the most difficult tasks. A copy editor named Fred McMorrow taught me much about sentences. But it was Paul Sann, then the executive editor, who most clearly fit the role of mentor. He could be corrosive when I was lousy. He could give hints of praise when I was good. He put me alongside more experienced writers so that I could learn more swiftly. He let me write multipart series of articles. He made me a columnist. He sent me to Vietnam and to riots and to political conventions. He even loaned me money. I suppose he was a mentor, but I thought of him as my friend.

He once told me, "If you have the story, tell it. If you don't have the story, *write* it." He urged me to read good writers and to analyze why they were good. "If you don't read, you'll never write," he said. "And if you read good writers, you have at least a chance of writing well yourself." He also warned me that the newspaper business was certain to break my heart. It did, and I didn't care. The run had been very long and very sweet.

In the end, a mentor can only move you part of the way to your goal. The mentor cannot accompany a person every hour of the day; we need guidance but not guardian angels. To get through an entire life, each of us must develop a secret mentor, hidden, private, living in our minds and imaginations. That personal mentor can be a composite of a number of people, those we know and those we have never met. But that mentor of the self must be rigorous, stern, compassionate, just, and also have a sense of humor. We are all capable of folly; it is, alas, part of being human. And the truly great mentor—real or imagined—is also forgiving. We might, on occasion, be required to forgive our friends and our enemies; our parents and our siblings; our spouses and our lovers; the luckiest of us might never have the need to do so. But we will always have a need to forgive ourselves. If that doesn't happen, if we make no mistakes, if we are more perfect than saints, then we will not have lived a life. The hidden, secret mentor in each of us must be in charge of taking responsibility for mistakes, forgiving them, and then starting again in the morning.

One final thing: if you are a young person who cannot find a real flesh-and-blood mentor, do not despair. There are literally thousands of mentors to choose from and all of them can be found in the public library. Every library is a temple of human wisdom. On the shelves, in those books, is the tale of the world with all its villains and heroes. Choose the company of heroes. Read the *Meditations* of Marcus Aurelius. Read the letters of Seneca, *The Count of Monte Cristo.* Ride with Don Quixote. Sail with Ulysses. Hear the tales of the Arabian nights. Go in and meet Albert Camus, whose father died when he was two months old. His mother could not read or write, and they lived in the grim slums of Oran in North Africa, and she never read a word her son wrote. But Camus won the Nobel Prize in literature when he was forty-two. Don't let anyone tell you that you can't walk the streets with Albert Camus beside you. Read him. Read about Jack Roosevelt Robinson, and what he did in the summer of 1947. And reach for a copy of Aristotle's *Ethics,* too. They are all waiting for your arrival.

KITTY CARLISLE HART

Kitty Carlisle Hart is chairman emeritus of the New York State Council on the Arts. She served as chairman from 1976 until 1996 and is the third person to occupy the post since the council's founding in 1960.

Mrs. Hart is an actress and singer with a long record of achievement in the arts and public service. She was born in New Orleans and educated in Europe—she attended school in Switzerland and went to the Sorbonne and the London School of Economics. She also studied acting in London at the Royal Academy of Dramatic Art.

While participating in a wide range of public service activities, Mrs. Hart has taken a particular interest in the role of women in society. She chaired the Statewide Conference of Women and was later appointed special consultant to Governor Nelson Rockefeller on women's opportunities.

Mrs. Hart was married to Pulitzer Prize–winning playwright and director Moss Hart, who died in 1961.

I WENT TO HOLLYWOOD to try to become a movie star, but I didn't feel that I was movie star material and also felt that no one was particularly interested in me. So I returned to New York, defeated.

Then I met Moss Hart. He was a wonderful and brilliant man. We had been married only a short time and he was working on a film that would become *Gentleman's Agreement,* with Gregory Peck. He was to finish writing the script in Hollywood. We were staying at Otto Preminger's house and going to a big Hollywood party that evening. Since I didn't do so well in my first foray into Hollywood, I was leery of going back. It frightened me because it seemed to reinforce my feelings of failure.

Before we went to the party, Moss sat me down in our room. "All your life you've been living under a cloak labeled Kitty Carlisle," he said. "And you keep the cloak over you because you feel no one wants to know who Kitty Carlisle is." He asked, "Do you know how wrong you are?" He went on to tell me that when we went to the party, he was going to leave me at the door. "If we stay with each other, we won't have anything to talk about when we get home." We went to the party and Moss left me on my own for the entire evening. I had a wonderful time. He had proven his point.

That evening became a turning point in my life. Moss really taught me the value of being myself. He gave me the desire to remove the cloak I was hiding under and let people see me. He showed me that people were genuinely interested in me. Most of all, I gained a new sense of self-worth, and it made such a difference.

I felt that I was married to a genius, and anything he did was fine by me. We had such fun together. And such growth. Moss Hart was always an inspiration for me. I learned so many valuable lessons from him and feel blessed that we were able to share so much of our lives together. I love him very much.

THEODORE M. HESBURGH

UNIVERSITY OF NOTRE DAME

Rev. Theodore M. Hesburgh, C.S.C., was educated at the University of Notre Dame and the Gregorian University in Rome. He was ordained in 1943 and received his doctorate in 1945. He joined Notre Dame's religion department that year and was appointed its head in 1948. He was named the fifteenth president of Notre Dame in June 1952, at the age of thirty-five.

Father Hesburgh stepped down as head of Notre Dame on June 1, 1987. He now spends his days at Notre Dame guest lecturing, presiding over liturgies, and advancing the interest of several university institutes.

He has remained a leader in the field of education and held fifteen presidential appointments which have involved him in major social issue such as civil rights, campus unrest, and immigration reform. His stature as an elder statesman in American higher education is reflected in his 138 honorary degrees, the most ever awarded to one person.

His awards include the Medal of Freedom, the nation's highest civilian honor, and the Meiklejohn Award of the American Association of University Professors. He is also a fellow of the American Academy of Arts and Sciences and a member of the American Philosophical Society.

MY MENTORING CAME AS AN ADULT rather than as a child. While my main mentors as a child were my parents, Theodore and Ann Marie (Murphy) Hesburgh, I was also greatly aided by our local parish priest, Father Harold Quinn. Their advice was always sound, and thank God I followed it.

When I was still a young man I had just passed my thirty-second birthday in 1949, the then president of the University of Notre Dame, Father Jim Cavanaugh, C.S.C., appointed me executive vice president of the university. I felt totally unprepared for this top executive position, so I asked him what was it really about. He responded, "It is only about administration."

I asked him, "What is administration all about?"

He replied quite casually, "It is about making decisions."

I then asked, "Well, how does one make good decisions?"

His response was quite simple: "You don't make decisions because you are deciding something that is easy to do. You don't make them because they are going to be popular and make you popular. You don't make them because they are not going to cost something, monetarily and personally. You simply make them because your decision is the right thing to do, no matter what the cost, no matter how unpopular it might make you, no matter how easy it is to do."

During the next three years, Father Cavanaugh exemplified this advice. He made a lot of difficult decisions, including some that cost him a good deal of popularity. He also made decisions that were fairly expensive compared to other ones. He put me in a position where I had to make similar decisions and he monitored them personally, since I generally passed them by him before making them. All in all, it was a great three-year experience.

In 1952 I was named president of the university at the age of thirty-five. Again, it seemed like an almost impossible task. The monitoring I received was enormously helpful, and I must say that it kept me out of trouble during the next thirty-five years I was president. Life would have been a lot more difficult without that good advice from my mentor, Father John. I have been eternally grateful to him—for both his good advice and his good example that exemplified his advice.

He had one other piece of advice which I have never forgotten: there is no leadership without vision. When you begin a difficult task, you must have a vision of where you are going—decisions are the way you get there. Again, this was mentoring of exceptional value. I would hope that everyone may have equally good mentoring before beginning a difficult task. It is also enormously helpful if the one who mentors you exemplifies what he is advising.

ANNE JACKSON

Anne Jackson made her debut in Eva Le Gallienne's production of *The Cherry Orchard*. She then became a member of the American Repertory Company, founded by LeGallienne and Webster and Cheryl Crawford. Her first commercial hit was in Tennessee Williams's *Summer and Smoke,* for which she received a Tony nomination. *Oh Men, Oh Women* earned her her second Tony nomination, which was quickly followed by a third nomination for *Middle of the Night,* by Paddy Chayefsky.

In subsequent years she has appeared in many Broadway plays with her husband Eli Wallach: *Major Barbara, Luv, Promenade All,* and *Waltz of the Toreadors.*

She is a charter member of the Actors' Studio and performs a poetry and literature evening with Eli Wallach which she and Wallach arranged. She has written a childhood memoir and biography, *Early Stages,* and is a doctor of fine arts at Southampton College.

MISS EDWARDS WAS A MIDDLE-AGED English teacher in junior high school, P.S. 171, who had an enormous influence on my early development. She gave me monologues to perform in assembly. I would stay after school and she would direct me in pieces such as the monologue from *Anne of Green Gables.* At this time my mother was in a mental hospital—I was only twelve or thirteen—so it was important to have this dear, caring woman in my life.

She taught me the value of sense memory (an acting technique used to emphasize emotional realism), although she didn't call it that. She simply saw memory as a facet of the power of the imagination. For instance, I would sit on a stationary chair in the classroom pretending I was riding a horse-drawn carriage with Mr. Cuthbert, one of the characters from *Anne of Green Gables.* Miss Edwards made sure that I rocked back and forth and actually "saw" trees, "felt" breezes, and "talked with" Mr. Cuthbert.

Miss Edwards helped me realize my strength as an actress. Five years later I performed the monologue from *Anne of Green Gables* on the stage of the John Golden Theater in Chicago. This got me my first job in the road company of Anton Chekhov's *The Cherry Orchard* with Eva LeGallienne, who was a major star of the theater in the 1940s and '50s.

She helped me to set my course, and I've been an actress ever since. I've had many kind adults, both male and female, assist me in the course of my career, but I believe that it was Miss Edwards who was most important to me.

Today, I teach actors and learn as much from them as they learn from me. That, to me, is the beauty of teaching. Helping others brings a great amount of pride and enjoyment, whether you are an adult or a child. Each of us must have the capacity to learn and continue to learn. Growth is always inspiring.

TANIA MARA

JAMES EARL JONES

Celebrated actor James Earl Jones is known for his powerful and critically acclaimed motion picture, television, and theater performances. His performance in the Alan Paton classic *Cry, The Beloved Country,* promises to remain in the annals of acting studies that will be researched by students of the art throughout the years. He has been praised by critics for his award-winning performance in *A Family Thing,* a strong human drama which pairs him with Robert Duvall. For all of his success in television and the movies, Jones's beginnings are in the theater.

He earned worldwide acclaim and his first Tony Award in the role of Jack Johnson, the first heavyweight boxing champion in Howard Sackler's *The Great White Hope.* His second Tony came as a result of his stunning performance in August Wilson's play *Fences.* He has also received critical praise for his autobiography *James Earl Jones: Voices and Silences,* which he coauthored with Penelope Niven.

First of all, let me say that I don't believe in mentors. That is, I don't believe that people can set out to be role models; if they do, it is usually somewhat false, and it doesn't work. For instance, a parent can't just decide to be a role model for his or her child. When such a relationship does exist, it usually just happens, because that child sees something in his role model which he responds to positively, which helps him search within himself to find his own potential.

I was raised by my grandparents, and I would say that my grandfather was, and still is, my hero. Outside of the family, my most influential role model was a high school English teacher, Donald Crouch. Professor Crouch was a former college teacher who had worked with Robert Frost, among others. He had retired to a farm near the small Michigan town where I lived, but when he discovered that there was a need for good teachers locally, he came to teach at my small agricultural high school.

Growing up, I had a hard time speaking because I was a stutterer, and felt self-conscious. Professor Crouch discovered that I wrote poetry, a secret I was not anxious to divulge, being a typical high school boy. After learning this, he questioned me about why, if I loved words so much, couldn't I say them outloud? One day I showed him a poem I had written, and he responded to it by saying that it was too good to be my own work, that I must have copied it from someone. To prove that I hadn't plagiarized it, he wanted me to recite the poem, by heart, in front of the entire class. I did as he asked, got through it without stuttering, and from then on I had to write more, and speak more. This had a tremendous effect on me, and my confidence grew as I learned to express myself comfortably outloud.

On the last day of school, we had our final class outside on the lawn, and Professor Crouch presented me with a gift—a copy of Ralph Waldo Emerson's *Self-Reliance.* This was invaluable to me because it summed up what he had taught me—self-reliance. His influence on me was so basic that it extended to all areas of my life.

He is the reason I became an actor. Several years later I was in Shakespeare's *Timon of Athens* at the Yale Repertory Theater.

Of course, Professor Crouch was the one person I knew I definitely had to invite, and so I asked him to come see me. By that time, though, he was almost completely blind, and said that he would rather not come if he couldn't see me. This was a disappointment, but I understood why he didn't want to come, and knew that he was right. In terms of overall influence, he is still the most important person outside my family whose inspiration has helped and guided me over the years.

Thomas H. Kean

As governor of New Jersey from 1982 to 1990, Thomas H. Kean was rated among America's five most effective governors by *Newsweek*. He was noted for tax cuts that spurred seven hundred fifty thousand new jobs, a federally replicated welfare reform program, landmark environmental policies, and over thirty education reforms. He also delivered the keynote address at the 1988 Republican National Convention.

Currently, as president of Drew University, Kean is shaping this school into one of the nation's leading small universities. He stresses the primacy of teaching, the creative use of technology in the liberal arts, and the importance of international education. He has also created a $10,000 award for outstanding teaching, a $2 million fund for minority scholarships, and a middle-income scholarship award.

THOMAS H. KEAN

Kean is the author of *The Politics of Inclusion.* He writes a bimonthly column for the *Bergen Record* and appears as a regular commentator on New Jersey network news.

WHEN I WAS IN SCHOOL, I was mildly dyslexic. But at the time, they really didn't know what it was or how it could be treated. I also had a bad stutter and a really difficult time getting words out. For fear of being ridiculed for my stutter, I pretty much avoided talking in class, and would sit in the back of the classroom and act ignorant. I was a mess.

I had a Latin teacher, William Gaccon, who took the time to help me in the afternoon. He helped me work out my problems by giving me a sense of self-confidence and convincing me that I had something to contribute not only to my classes but to a greater good as well. With his help, my stutter improved and I became a better student. Everyone who knew me was amazed by my transformation. Between the ages of eleven and fifteen it seemed inconceivable that I would succeed, but by my junior year in high school I had gone from being a poor student to being a good one. None of this would have happened without the help of Mr. Gaccon. Our friendship continued over the course of our careers and lasted until his death several years ago.

Another influential factor in my adolescence was my experience at a summer camp in New Hampshire for underprivileged children. At that camp people from different backgrounds became my lifelong friends. I started volunteering when I was sixteen and was given responsibilities way beyond my years. As counselors, we were taught to be mentors. I returned each summer of my high school and college years and ultimately ended up running the camp.

The camp played a large role in my life. I found I could help kids who had problems similar to the ones I faced in my early school years. Many of the campers returned as counselors because they wanted to help others in much the same way.

Every now and again I receive letter from former campers telling me how positive their camp experience had been. Most of these kids grew up to become successful in the careers they chose. At one camp reunion, a former camper told of returning to his old neighborhood in Charleston, a suburb of Boston, only to find that most of his friends from his old neighborhood were either dead or in jail. He had come to the reunion just to say thank you, to no one in particular, but more to the camp itself, simply for being there for him. He felt it had saved his life.

It is a lot more difficult for kids these days. There is so much more out there that is against them. I wish there was a single simple solution to solve the problems facing our nation's children, but there isn't. All I can offer is what I know that works. Mentoring kids—taking time out for them—works. It worked for me. And I have seen it work for so many others. I am a total believer in mentoring because I have seen it change lives, including my own.

ANDREW ECCLES © 1997 CNN

LARRY KING

Larry King has been in the interviewing business for over forty years. He hosts CNN's *Larry King Live,* the only live worldwide phone-in television talk show, as well as the network's highest rated program, *Larry King Weekend,* and a series of specials for Turner Network Television. In addition, he writes a weekly newspaper column for *USA Today* and has written eleven books.

King has been inducted into five of the leading Broadcasters' Hall of Fame, has won the George Foster Peabody Award for excellence in broadcasting, and won ten Cable ACE Awards for best interviewer and for Best talk show series. In 1997 he celebrated his fortieth anniversary in the broadcasting industry and received a star on the Hollywood Walk of Fame.

King founded the Larry King Cardiac Foundation and is also involved with the American Heart Association and the Save the Children Foundation.

WHEN I WAS A CHILD, all I wanted to do was be on the radio, and there were two great radio broadcasters who influenced me and whom I admired. Arthur Godfrey was a wonderful broadcaster who exemplified great values—he was a risk taker, had a great personality, and above all, he was always himself. Red Barber was a Dodger announcer whom I not only listened to as a child, but also tried to imitate. I can remember pretending to be him when I was about ten years old, doing imaginary sports broadcasts by myself. I later met and worked with both these men, which was like living out a dream.

Both of these men had an enormous influence on my career as a radio broadcaster, for they taught me several important lessons. From them, I learned to be myself, and to take risks. They showed me that in our profession, the only secret is that there is no secret, and that above all I should trust my instincts. They gave me simple advice—to be the best I could be.

On a personal level, there were several people who had a tremendous effect on my life. Mario Cuomo, through his brilliance and friendship, taught me the importance of having a strong character. One of my favorite people has been Stan Musial, a baseball player. However, one individual who had an enormous influence on me was Edward Bennett Williams, a genius in the courtroom and a wonderful friend and adviser. Just being in his presence had a strong effect on me. Above all, he exemplified truthfulness and taught me that it was no shame to show one's feelings.

There is one moment I shared with Edward that has stayed with me for the past ten years. I was walking with him down Connecticut Avenue two weeks before he died of cancer, and he knew he was going to die. He was cheering me up, telling me what a great career I had, and what a wonderful life. I asked him, "Aren't you scared?"

He was a devout Catholic, had always gone to church regularly, and he replied that if this life was all there was, then it didn't make any sense, and everything was just one big cosmic joke. Why do anything, he asked. Why work? In his mind, there had to be something greater than our life on earth, and he accepted this calmly. This concept was much more logical to him than the idea that there was nothing. I'm an agnostic, and his words had a tremendous impact on me. I can still hear his voice, saying those words.

Another great friend whom I have known since we were nine, is Herb Cohen. Herbie taught me that you can negotiate anything. He would get me in trouble, and then get me out of it again. When we were seventeen years old, we were walking one night when a squad car pulled up next to us. The police began questioning both of us about a series of robberies that had recently occurred, for we fit the description of the robbers. I immediately started to cry; Herbie, on the other hand, confessed to the crimes. He thought it would be fun to take a trip to the police station. He was crazy then, and is still crazy now, and I consider him my closest friend.

Paul Newman told me once that anyone who had gotten anywhere and doesn't acknowledge the influence of luck is fooling himself. I was lucky enough to be born with some talent, and I had the ability to pursue my dream, but much of my success can only be contributed to luck. However, the influence of the friends and advisers I have had throughout the years has strengthened and helped me along the way.

From the relationships I have had with these men, I have seen that circumstances change, but that people never do. You don't lie to your friends, for friendship is one of the most valuable things you can have. One is lucky to have even one good friend, and I have been lucky enough to have three or four, Herb being the closest.

The fact that all of these role models, both personal and professional, were outside of my immediate family, made a great difference in my life. My father died when I was nine and a half, and so an older male influence was very important to me. I was raised by a strong loving mother and had a younger brother, but these key people outside of my family gave me support of a different kind.

The four men I have mentioned had a collective impact on me, teaching several important lessons through their examples or their friendship. They taught me to never be afraid to take a risk, never cop out on my values, never lie to a friend, and, above all, that all things will pass. I am a commentator, not a brain surgeon. I do not save people's lives. Knowing that I am not more important than anyone else, that I go on the air at nine o'clock and then off again at ten really puts things in perspective. This kind of awareness is important to anyone who has risen to prominence in their chosen career, for falling down can be much harder than rising up.

WILLIAM G. HARRIS

Mathilde Krim

Soon after the first cases of AIDS were reported in 1981, Dr. Mathilde Krim recognized that the new disease raised grave scientific and medical questions and that it might have important sociopolitical consequences. In 1983, she founded the AIDS Medical Foundation, the first private organization concerned with fostering and supporting AIDS research. In 1985, AMF merged with a like-minded group based in California to form the American Foundation for AIDS research (AmFAR). Dr. Krim is AmFAR's founding cochair and currently chairman of the board.

In 1953, Dr. Krim received her Ph.D. from the University of Geneva, Switzerland. From 1953 to 1959 she pursued research in cytogenetics and cancer-causing viruses at the Weizmann Institute of Science in Israel, where she was a member of the team that first developed a method for the prenatal determination of sex.

I WAS ONE OF THOSE LUCKY CHILDREN who grew up in a nurturing, cohesive, and extended—almost clannish—family, which included two parents, four grandparents, and many other relatives. And yet, I always yearned to explore beyond the family circle because I felt a need to break out and compare members of my family to others. I did experience the important and positive help of mentors, but only starting in my teens and young adult years.

One of my mentors was a stern and demanding, but inspiring Latin and history teacher. In two years of high school, he taught me the disciplines of logical thinking and writing. To date, I remember Mr. Chevalier's words and face, his demeanor and smile, and his ability to inspire intellectual delight. He also helped me find relieving humor in the course of stern lectures. There was also a female English teacher whom we, in an all-girls high school, dreaded, but whose love of English literature was so winning and contagious that I came to love and admire her greatly. These two individuals taught me a lot about setting personal standards of performance. And being able to live up to the expectations of such individuals greatly helped my self-esteem in my teenage years.

Throughout the years, various mentors have entered my life for short or extended periods of time. Some have been older friends, teachers, or senior professional colleagues. They all have broadened the frame of reference provided by my original family, and they have helped me to compare notes, to assent or argue with them, and, in total, to think for myself, break out of a preordained mold, and find my own way in society.

What they all had in common was that they were freely chosen by me to be attentive, respectful of me, and older. Each in one way or another was an anchor at some time in my life, somebody whom I could hold on to in case of need, who would listen to me and respond honestly. In that sense, each was a true mentor.

CHUENG CHING MING

MAYA LIN

Maya Lin has won international acclaim for her site-specific art and architecture projects. Since her design for the Vietnam Veterans' Memorial in Washington, D.C., Ms. Lin has continued to establish herself in both the art and architecture communities. Her unique sensitivity to landscape and topography, as well as her ability to create meditative and contemplative places in highly public spaces, is evident in her works, including the Wave Field, an earthwork at the University of Michigan, the Weber Residence in Williamstown, Massachusetts, the Museum for African Art in New York, and the water tables of the Civil Rights Memorial and the Women's Table at Yale University.

She has been the recipient of numerous awards and honorary doctorates and been featured in publications around the world. Her current projects include sculpture installations for the Cleveland Public Library, Stanford University, and two private collections. Her architectural commissions include the Asia/Pacific/American Studies Department at New York University and a library and chapel for the Children's Defense Fund at Haley Farm in Clinton, Tennessee. Her solo exhibition, Maya Lin: Topologies, will tour the country throughout the year.

MY BROTHER AND I GREW UP in Athens, Ohio, where my parents worked as professors at Ohio University. They had recently immigrated from China, which isolated us from the community, but which also created a unique closeness within our family.

I learned a lot from my mother and father, perhaps more than other children do from their parents. In China there is an emphasis on the family serving as the primary mentors. This was certainly true for my family.

Each member of my family has been a creative influence. My father was a ceramist, my mother is a writer, my brother a poet. Our closeness as a family seemed to fuel our own artistic natures—we were always learning from and inspired by one another. My approach to architecture was very much influenced by my father's methods as a ceramist. When making models I frequently use a material called plasticine. It is a claylike substance that does not dry or harden, and allows me to continously mold and shape the material. It is a direct influence from my father.

I was very fortunate in my early education. From the first to sixth grade I went to a school where the student-teacher ratio was very much in the favor of the students. There was one teacher for every twelve or thirteen children, allowing the teachers to address the needs of each student on a personal basis. My art and chemistry teachers are individuals I still keep in touch with today.

I have had two great teachers in my education at Yale University. Professor Vincent Scully was a critical influence on my thoughts of architecture as a social and personal practice. I studied under him as an undergraduate, also serving as a teacher's assistant while I was in graduate school. Professor Scully really directed my thoughts on the way architecture shapes how we feel and experience a place. I began questioning how my work would affect people. How would people feel when they saw my work? What was I trying to express to them? These became key questions I ask in my approach to each project. I would begin at the end, understanding the effect I was hoping to convey, and work to develop the technical means to produce this effect.

Frank Gehry, a visiting professor at the graduate school of architecture, was also a very strong influence on my work. He was the only person who told me not to worry about whether I was an artist or an architect, telling me that my work crossed over boundaries and that I shouldn't worry about the distinctions. It was advice that has helped me pursue a course that places me between the fields of art and architecture.

I am very lucky to have been influenced by my family as well as my teachers. My family has always been there for me, educating me artistically and personally. My teachers helped push me to think and view my work in various contexts. I would not be where I am today without them.

Sirio Maccioni

ANDREW BORDWIN

Sirio Maccioni has dedicated his life to the restaurant business and has achieved love and respect around the world as the founder of Le Cirque. Born in the Tuscan town of Montecatini Terme, Mr. Maccioni attendeed high school there before moving on to restaurant and hotel training programs in Paris, France, and Hamburg. After a series of apprenticeships in Montecatini and Paris, he held a variety of positions at hotels and restaurants in Italy, France, and Germany.

Eventually, Mr. Maccioni took his skills to sea with Home Lines before moving to the United States to continue his career. In March 1974 he realized a dream when he opened his own restaurant, Le Cirque. With his wife Egidiana at his side and three sons in tow, he created what quickly became New York City's most favored restaurant. The family hasn't had time to look back.

MY FATHER AND MOTHER were Italians from Tuscany who died during World War II. After their deaths my sister and I went to live with my grandmother, Nunzia, who stressed simplicity as a worthy goal in life. She was an intelligent woman who wanted us to do the best we could. "Don't wait," she would say. "Do something now." She tried to create my character early, and wanted people to feel at ease around us. From her I learned to be socially correct and proper. She must have foreseen my future line of work.

When I was seventeen, I had the opportunity to go to France. Once there I was helped a great deal by a fellow Italian who was also from Tuscany—the famous singer and actor Yves Montand. He was an extremely talented man, a man of conviction. He was also a very controversial figure at the time and accused of many things. He was even labeled a Communist because he went to Russia as a performer. But he also helped me in my early days in the restaurant industry. He helped me to survive in Paris by finding a job for me in a restaurant. I am very thankful to have known him.

If you wanted to work in the restaurant industry in Europe, it was necessary to know several languages. Being in Paris, I had learned French but I still needed German, so I moved to Germany and lived there long enough to learn the language. Then I had the chance to go to America.

I came to New York in 1956 after working on a luxury cruise liner as a waiter and dancer. I could not speak English, but someone helped me a great deal. Oscar Delmonico gave me my first job in New York and was instrumental in helping me enroll in a six-month English course at Hunter College. I was going to school during the day and working in the restaurant at night. It was not the steadiest of jobs—I was mainly a replacement when other employees could not come in—but it helped me with the bills.

I received my green card in 1958 and began working at the Colony Restaurant on 61st Street in Manhattan, which was owned by the Cavalerro family. Soon I realized I knew all the customers. I had met many of them when I was working in Europe, and now I could speak whatever language they spoke; I was very qualified. I was soon promoted to be the temporary head of the Colony and was written up in *Life* magazine.

In 1974, with the help of the Zeckendorf family, who managed the Mayfair Hotel on East 65th Street, I opened a new restaurant called Le Cirque. Mr. Zeckendorf took a chance with me because he believed in me. I ran Le Cirque from 1974 until June 1996, then I moved to the Villard Houses on 455 Madison Avenue and re-opened the restaurant as Le Cirque 2000 on May 1, 1997.

I would like to thank all the people who have helped me in my work. I have met all of the most important people in the United States and many world leaders. I knew President Kennedy and his parents. I think he was a nice man and a good president. My family and I were shocked when he was killed. I also knew President Nixon personally. He was nice to my family and even advised my sons about their college education, especially since I really did not know much about colleges and universities.

Of all the things I have learned, one of the most important is to have an open mind and respect people, but stick to your convictions.

I have a great wife. She was a famous singer in Italy and also had a show at Carnegie Hall in New York. Together we have three sons: Mario, Marco, and Mauro. We all speak three languages fluently. They all went to good schools; I made sure that they had a great education. I wanted a doctor, lawyer, or a president—but they all work with me selling soup.

My dream in life is to have a good home and a good family. My work has been successful, and I have been able to be at home in Tuscany and New York. My entire family meets in Italy as often as we can, but always in summer. I have fulfilled this dream. I just always want to be together with my family and, of course, have great food.

HOWARD S. MAIER

Howard S. Maier is president of Maier Ventures, a marketing company with headquarters in Great Neck, New York. He is also the president of Yoga Zone LLC, a chain of yoga studios in the New York metropolitan area.

Before establishing Maier Ventures, Mr. Maier was president of the Maier Group, which he sold to Time-Warner in 1994. The Maier Group was a producer of nontheatrical videos and was the country's leading marketer of exercise videos, most notably the *Buns of Steel* series. The Maier Group ranked on INC. 500's list of the fastest-growing private companies for four successive years (1991–94). Mr. Maier was a 1993 Entrepreneur of the Year finalist.

Mr. Maier devotes significant time to charitable organizations. He sits on the board of overseers of the Boas/Marks Research Center and is an associate trustee of North Shore/Long Island Jewish Hospital. He received a B.S. from the State University of New York (SUNY) at Buffalo in 1968 and an M.B.A. from the Bernard M. Baruch Graduate School of Business in 1972.

SAM STRYKER WAS MY FIRST BOSS at Clairol. He taught me motivational and marketing skills that enabled me to eventually become a successful entrepreneur. Sam emphasized the importance of teamwork and motivation to achieve success. This proved to work for me, both in the corporate world and as an entrepreneur.

The division of labor in large business organizations is vast and very detail-oriented. Sam Stryker saw the need to get employees to respond to the needs of the organization in which they worked. The trick of leadership lies in motivating employees to perform specific tasks which, along with the tasks of others, combine to form the finished product of that business.

Sam believed it was important to turn people on to your project. You also had to know how to turn a negative situation into a positive result. He knew the importance of positive motivation. His philosophy of a business's success paralleled that of Sam Walton: you emulate what people do well and try to change what they don't do well. You try to improve on their particular drawbacks and then attempt to transform them into strengths.

One way to achieve this result lay in training. Although marketing is an art, one must still learn basic skills. Sam took the time to train me in marketing operations as well as employee motivation.

Another key component of Stryker's philosophy was to put the company above the individual. Again, this is part of his teamwork mentality. Sam believed in the value of camaraderie inside and outside the office as a strengthening agent for the business itself. He saw this as relevant to dealing with people and motivating them. The statement "It's not me, it's we" has also become a valuable standard for me. In my business, I have always viewed my success as *our* success. I, too, incorporate this belief, whether I am sending parents a baby gift or taking employees to a New York Knicks game. People will respond to you much better if they feel you care about them.

Sam Stryker took me at a relatively young age and guided me in how to get things done. His philosophy helped me become successful.

JACK GESCHEIDT

PETER MAX

Peter Max is one of the most important artists of our time. From visionary pop artist of the 1960s to new-expressionistic painter, Max's vibrant color palette and bold graphic imagery have become so much a part of contemporary American culture that his influence in art has often been compared to the Beatles' influence in music.

Max has been designated as the official artist for five Super Bowls, five Grammy Awards shows, the U.S. Open, the World Cup soccer games, the fiftieth anniversary of the United Nations, and numerous other international events.

As a painter for the last five U.S. presidents and through his annual tradition of painting the Statue of Liberty, Max has earned the reputation of "America's painter laureate." His many posters for peace, the environment, and human and animal rights have also earned him a reputation as "America's environmental artist."

Peter Max's fascination with the new digital technology in the age of the Internet is inspiring him to become the cyber artist for the new millennium, with his website, www.petermax.com as his latest "canvas."

WHEN I WAS YOUNG, I didn't want to be a painter. I spent my first ten years in Shanghai, China, and the country itself served as my first mentor. I was this small Caucasian boy, an only child, surrounded by this amazing eight thousand-year-old Oriental influence.

I became fascinated with the holy people of Shanghai. I would see Buddhist monks on my way to school every morning. You would look in their eyes and just see an ocean of calm. I also got to know the street artists. They were like monks in the way they renounced the material things of the world. They lived on the streets of the city and created beautiful art. I saw Buddhist sand paintings for the first time in Shanghai and am still fascinated by them today.

The street artist inspired me, and I started drawing and painting as a child in China. I had a nanny, Uma, who would draw with me in the garden surrounding three-quarters of my family's three-tiered pagoda house. She taught me to hold my brush in the Oriental way. Uma also bought me these small colorful posters illustrated with traditional Chinese stories. I loved the intricate color arrangements found in these different art forms. Their influence would later show up in my work.

Being an only child, I was also enormously influenced by my parents. I remember walking with my father to the store one day and seeing a street vendor sitting on an orange crate. He had small bundles of what appeared to be newspapers. Upon closer inspection, they turned out to be American comic books. My dad bought these bundles for me, and for the next several weeks, I devoured them. I loved the outlines of the comic books, the sense of geometry and borders, and their color schemes. Quite unknowingly, I related color to a sense of atmosphere, of mood, that relayed the themes of the stories. Somehow all this clicked with comics.

Comics led to a fascination with American movies. I remember the first time I heard the word *director* and asked what it meant. It was then that I made the connection that this magical stuff in the movies was from someone's mind. It was a creation. It was someone's story.

All this Americana, including jazz, were like seeds that would slowly germinate for me. When my family moved to Brooklyn in 1953, I became fascinated with astronomy in high school. I loved the concepts of space and stars existing light years away. I loved the concept of infinity. I thought I would be an astronomer. I was excellent at math and really lucky with several teachers who encouraged my enthusiasm. At the same time, I continued drawing and painting. I started drawing stars, and then began with some of the monks I had seen in China. My parents were so supportive of me. My mom made the biggest fuss over anything I did, and my peers were supportive as well. This made me work twice as hard.

Over the years I found my own style and visual ways to tell my own stories. I strive to do just that. But I wouldn't be where I am today without the life I have led so far and the various influences I have had.

Carolyn McCarthy

OFFICIAL HOUSE OF REPRESENTATIVES PHOTO

Carolyn McCarthy is a lifelong resident of Mineola, New York, in the heart of the Fourth Congressional District. A licensed practical nurse, Mrs. McCarthy has over thirty years of experience working in the health care field. She married Dennis McCarthy in 1967 and they raised one son, Kevin.

Mrs. McCarthy led a mostly quiet life as a nurse and housewife until she was thrust into the spotlight on December 7, 1993. After her husband was killed and her son injured during the Long Island Railroad Massacre, Carolyn McCarthy turned her tragedy into a public campaign against gun violence. She advocates providing all children with a good education and an opportunity to attend college, creating safe and drug-free schools, cutting down on drug use, and creating more job opportunities to pay a living wage.

She was elected to the House of Representatives on November 7, 1996. She had never run for political office before.

WHEN I WAS A CHILD, I spent a lot of time with my Aunt Helen. She was a schoolteacher in Brooklyn and the first person to notice that I had trouble learning. She began to spend the summers with me, teaching me how to read and encouraging me to learn. It was because of her attention that my parents finally discovered my dyslexia. Before I was diagnosed, I thought I couldn't read because I was stupid. But Aunt Helen showed me that I was an intelligent girl who just needed to work hard and study more.

It would be difficult to single out one specific experience with Aunt Helen. I was a little girl and every moment with her seemed special. Whether it was reading together or visiting her school, little by little she gave me confidence in myself. She told me over and over again that I was smart and could accomplish anything with a little hard work. As I spent time with her, I began doing other things, like playing sports and making new friends. Years later I even heard her voice inside of me when I decided to run for Congress.

I was also able to give my son Kevin help because of the support I received from my Aunt Helen, when we discovered that he, too, had a learning disability. And after the Long Island Railroad incident, I had the self-confidence to go door-to-door and talk to complete strangers about the very serious issue of gun violence, and ultimately run for Congress.

Overall, the most valuable lesson Aunt Helen taught me is the importance of positive thinking. She was always positive, which made a world of difference. Now, when I visit schools and talk to students, I tell them not to let anyone discourage them from doing something. I strongly feel that a person can accomplish anything if they set their mind to it.

There was also another individual in my life whom I consider a mentor. When I was nineteen years old, I dated a young man who was in a fatal car accident. The nurse who took care of him before his death taught me what it truly means to help someone in need. After spending time with this courageous woman, I decided to pursue a nursing career.

If you tell a child enough times that they are smart and that they can do something, they start to believe they can. Every child should set high goals, and it is our responsibility as adults to encourage and support their dreams. I don't think Aunt Helen really knew the impact she would have on my life, so I hope this book is a reminder to all mentors that they are truly making a difference.

STAN RUNBOUGH

DINA MERRILL

Dina Merrill has starred in film, and on Broadway and television. She suspended her career for several years while she took time off to marry and have children. When they were old enough, she returned to work and hasn't stopped since.

Dina has been described as a Republican with a democratic heart. She devotes a great deal of her time to working for the disadvantaged. When one of her children was diagnosed as diabetic, Dina became one of the founders of the Juvenile Diabetes Foundation. On the artistic side, she is a trustee of the Eugene O'Neill Theater Center and a director of the Museum of Broadcasting. She was a presidential appointee to the board of trustees of the John F. Kennedy Center for the Performing Arts. She is also a director of Project Orbis, a flying eye hospital which teaches advanced eye care and surgical techniques all over the world.

Her home base is divided between New York City and Los Angeles, the film production base for RKO Pictures, for which she is vice chairman.

I NEVER REALLY HAD AN ADULT MENTOR when I was very young. The closest I came occurred in a one-time experience when I had turned twelve and Walter Houston was visiting my family in the Adirondacks. We went for a walk one day and he asked what I wanted to do when I grew up. I told him I wanted to be an actress. He said, "Got any Shakespeare plays handy?" I found a copy of *Twelfth Night* and we read several scenes together the next day. He made suggestions and we read again and again. I was overwhelmed that he would take the time to do that with me.

When I was in my twenties, and married, I stopped working to have my kids. My husband and I met Dick Powell and June Allyson. One day Dick called and told me he was making his television debut on the Kate Smith show with a ten-minute scene. He said I was perfect for the girl opposite him and that he would recommend me to the producer. Thanks to him, I got the job.

Later, when he had the Four-Star Theater, Dick gave me several leading roles and helped me to become a television actress. He was someone I could always call when I had auditioned and didn't get the part; he would tell me what happened. I relied on him for that kind of input. He was always honest, which agents never are, and he knew what was going on in Hollywood. I don't know how I could have negotiated those first years in Los Angeles without him and his wife. He was a wonderful man, and June became the godmother for my second son, David.

JACK MITCHELL

MIDORI

Violinist Midori is one of the most celebrated figures in the music world. Her performing schedule takes her to the great concert stages of Europe, North America, and the Far East. In 1992 she added an important dimension to her public life when she established Midori and Friends (the Midori Foundation), whose educational programs seek to inspire children by bringing music into their everyday lives.

Her numerous releases on Sony Classical include a live recording of the Dvorak Violin Concerto with Zubin Mehta and the New York Philharmonic, and a recording of the Paganini Caprices for Solo Violin, nominated for a Grammy Award in 1990.

Midori was born in Osaka, Japan, in 1971, and began

studying the violin with her mother, Setsu Goto, at a very early age. In 1982, Zubin Mehta invited her to be a surprise guest soloist at the New York Philharmonic's traditional New Year's Eve concert, at which she received a standing ovation and the impetus to begin a major career.

THERE WERE PEOPLE WHO INSPIRED and encouraged me by their thoughts and actions in my personal as well as my public life. Perhaps some of them did not exactly fit the bill of mentor in the sense of being a teacher, but they exerted a strong influence—they supported, encouraged, and consoled me, and they still do so today.

Two of them are my closest friends. Two others are great artists—one living, the other now gone. One taught me that if I believe in something, I must act on it: Take the initiative and do not wait for others. Be involved; be active.

The other artist challenged me constantly and made me realize how important it is to think for myself and bear responsibility for what I do musically. He questioned everything, and opened my eyes to what was possible. When you are a soloist you must be fully aware of why you do what you do. Of course, music is deeply personal, but when you produce music without thinking, it is not your music. Your musical and artistic potential is not realized. Some musicians will disagree here on the theory that artistic merit springs from spontaneity, and in a way it does. We remember Thomas Edison's remark that "invention is 95 percent perspiration and 5 percent inspiration."

I believe that inspiration comes to you only after you understand the logic of what works and what does not. A house needs to be built on a solid foundation. A foundation of sand does not hold. An artist also needs a foundation based on sound thinking in order to be inspired and for that inspiration to be a success.

Now, about my two friends. I've known them both for a long time. One is a wonderful role model: she believes in herself and in what she does. On a daily basis, she reaches for the best within herself to give to her work and to others. She is always, always motivated to solve problems and achieve goals. She participates in life to her fullest capacity and shares herself generously with others.

My other close friend influenced me in a different way. He helped me to discover myself and to learn what was meaningful and truly important. In a busy world with demands from without and within, sometimes our inner feelings are left unheeded. This man was available to me, without an agenda of his own, when I most needed someone. He defined friendship and trust for me.

In terms of inspiration, I am revitalized again and again by the children I meet through my work with Midori and Friends. They allow me to share what I love and they accept whatever I offer. Our process of engaging is primal, personal, and valuable to me. It is always a pleasure and an honor to share what I have. Indeed, it is a privilege.

These people shaped my life. I cherish the inspiration they have given to me and to my work, and am grateful that our paths have crossed.

William D. Modell

William D. Modell is chairman of the board of Modell's Sporting Goods, a 109-year-old family-owned retail business, established in 1889. Headquartered in New York City, Modell's operates a chain of seventy-eight full-line sporting goods stores in New York's tri-state area, Pennsylvania, Maryland, Virginia, and Washington, D.C., with combined sales of $370 million.

In 1994, Modell was inducted into the National Sporting Goods Hall of Fame and one year later he was named Entrepreneur of the Year by the Entrepreneur Institute. *Crain's New York Business* awarded him its coveted All-Star Award in 1997.

He is the founder of the Long Island chapter of the Young Presidents Organization, the American Digestive Disease Society, the Gilda Radner Foundation, the Long Island City Business Development Corp, and the Seawane Country

Club. He is a cofounder of the Crohn's and Colitis Foundation of America, the Jeffrey Modell Foundation for Immunological Research, and the Hewlett House, a resource center for breast cancer survivors.

AS A YOUNGSTER, I thought my father, Henry, was perfect in every way. Yet it was my Uncle Harry who became my mentor and showed me how to find my own path to success.

I suppose that like most sons of successful fathers, I was in awe of my dad. He set high standards, and, looking back on my childhood, I do not think I ever believed that I could measure up to his standards of excellence. By the time I was eight or nine, I started to get in trouble at school. I suppose that some would say I was creating an excuse for failing to be the perfect son. At the time I thought I was being a free spirit. Whatever the reason, I began spending a lot of time in the principal's office. That is when Uncle Harry came into my life.

Harry Silverman, my uncle by marriage, was born in a tough neighborhood in South Philadelphia. The son of immigrants, Harry worked his way through the University of Pennsylvania at night and earned a degree in architecture. He loved his profession and took pride in his work. I don't know why, but Uncle Harry began to take me to his office on Saturdays.

As he worked, he would teach me about designing buildings, and, by example, he showed me how to organize my thinking process. At first he would give me fairly simple tasks, and I soon began to develop mental discipline and a new confidence. One of the greatest lessons that Uncle Harry taught me was that it was all right to make a mistake. He would tell me not to agonize over a mistake, but to learn from it and move on. The real turning point for me occurred when I began to realize that I did not have to be exactly like my father to achieve my dreams and succeed. Working with Uncle Harry, I learned that there was more than one way—sometimes even a better way—to conduct yourself in business and in life.

After the bombing of Pearl Harbor in 1941, the construction industry collapsed. Uncle Harry did not become bitter when he lost his job. Instead, he turned to my father and asked for a job. My dad hired him as the store manager of Modell's Sporting Goods 42nd Street store in the heart of Times Square. With no prior retail experience, Harry made it the chain's top store in volume of sales in just three months.

Not surprisingly, I followed Harry to the Times Square store, and worked there after school and on weekends. Through him, I developed a great love of retailing. I also learned why his friends and family called him straight-arrow. Uncle Harry's word was his bond. His integrity set a standard for everyone who worked for him, including me. To this day, when confronted with a moral decision, I ask myself how Harry would handle it. In most cases, I find the right answer.

My father was a brilliant and successful man. He succeeded his father, who founded the company in 1889 on the northeast corner of West and Cortlandt streets in Manhattan. I loved him and was incredibly proud of him. Yet it was Uncle Harry who showed me how to be my own man and succeed. He was the one who gave me the confidence to branch out and create one of the first mega-discount department store chains, Modell's Shopper's World, and later to begin a policy of regional expansion.

Today my sons are fourth-generation top executives at Modell's. As I mentor them, I try to emulate Uncle Harry: teach by example; allow everyone to make mistakes and learn from them; and be a straight-arrow. It has not always been easy to stand back and let my sons find their own way, but the results have been more rewarding than I ever dared to dream. I know Uncle Harry would be as proud of them as I am.

With warm memories of a truly wise man, I am proud to say, "Thanks, Uncle Harry."

Josie Natori with her grandmother, Josefa Almeda.

JOSIE NATORI

The year 1997 was dramatically exciting for Josie Natori: she celebrated her twentieth year in business, her twenty-fifth wedding anniversary, and her fiftieth birthday. She also achieved her lifelong dream of becoming an accomplished concert pianist with a brilliant performance at Carnegie Hall, where she performed with the Orchestra of St. Luke's to an international audience of family and friends.

In 1977, Mrs. Natori left a lucrative career on Wall Street to enter the world of fashion. What started as a company that made nightshirts with traditional Philippine embroidery blossomed into a full-scale fashion enterprise of elegant lingerie, accessories, at-home wear, and ready-to-wear.

In addition to running a business, she sits on the board

of trustees of Manhattanville College, the Asia Society, and the Asian Cultural Council. She serves on the board of directors of the Educational Foundation of Fashion Industries, the Philippine-American Foundation, and Junior Achievement, Inc. She is also a member of the World Presidents Organization, the Committee of two hundred, and the Council of Fashion Designers of America.

I WAS THE FIRST OF THIRTY-THREE GRANDCHILDREN and spent most of my summers with my grandmother, Josefa Almeda, in the province of Camarines Sur, in the Philippines. My grandmother was an amazing woman entrepreneur. She owned and operated businesses ranging from ice manufacturing plants and drug stores to movie theaters and plantations. She was a hands-on businesswoman. As a child, I would spend my days riding in a jeep around Naga City and its outskirts with my grandmother as she visited her businesses. We would rise at five o'clock in the morning and not stop until midnight. To me she seemed like the mayor of the town, traveling and holding court.

She was a strong woman—the mother of eight—who always stressed the importance of independence to me. She believed that women, even married, should have their own means of support and never have to depend on anyone or anything. She also believed that individuals controlled their own destiny. She was the personification of all she preached, which made quite an impression on me.

She taught me the value of self-discipline and the continuing need for self-improvement and education. I was always learning something, whether it was a foreign language, cooking, typing, or the arts. Her energy was my inspiration. She never stopped, and early on I decided to be as much like her as I could.

My grandmother was voracious about life. She said that you can't just talk about things you wanted to do, you had to act. Words were never enough for her. It was all about action, being tough on yourself and giving your all. She never complained and lived every minute of life to the fullest. Within her lifetime, I think she must have traveled to about 100 countries.

Even in her last years, she didn't let her battle with cancer get in her way. After a prolonged battle with the disease, she received the sacrament of last rites on her supposed deathbed. Everyone thought she was gone. I called her long distance and told her that she needed to get well so we could travel again. Miraculously, she improved and managed to travel to New York to spend time with me before we set out for a two-month tour of France and Spain. Every day her strength seemed to improve. All this after receiving last rites!

I think she knew that this was her last journey, but even then she refused to slow down. She died at eighty-nine, having lived life to the fullest more than anyone I have ever known. I feel blessed to have experienced it with her firsthand. To others she must have seemed a force of nature, which she was.

Another person from a completely opposite sphere that I feel blessed to have known was my piano tutor, Olga Stroumillo. I had taken piano lessons from the time I was four but I really didn't appreciate the beauty of music until I began studying with Madame Stroumillo. She was Russian, a best friend of Vladimir Horowitz, and earlier in her career, an assistant to Sergei Rachmaninov.

She was a very philosophical woman. She always told me that everything in life, like everything in music, is connected. To her, music was simply a metaphor for life itself, for the act and art of living. "Nothing is an accident," she would tell me. "One thing leads to another like fingers on the keys, like notes within the scales. Music is life."

Like my grandmother, Madame Stroumillo preached the need for self-discipline and being tough on yourself. She also spoke of the truth found within music and within yourself. To create something beautiful—in music or in life—you have to approach it from a place of truth. Truth is essential to both.

Madame Stroumillo lived the last years using a walker, barely able to care for herself. However, her brother was in much worse physical condition, and she was determined to move in with him.

When I pointed out her own ailing health, she responded with a smile that she had to care for both of them. She was determined to live longer than her brother because if she died first, he would have no one else. She did outlive him.

Both of these women were immensely important role models. They approached life with a sense of purpose and self-sufficiency and amazed people with their own acts of willpower and survival. I feel blessed to have had their encouragement and belief in me. I was always in awe of them. They enriched my life so that I feel they are still with me.

JANIE EISENBERG

JACK NEWFIELD

Jack Newfield is a columnist for the *New York Post*. He is also the author of six books and the writer or coproducer of four television documentaries, including *Robert Kennedy: A Memoir,* which appeared on the Discovery Channel in 1998.

Newfield has also won an Emmy for his documentary *Don King: Unauthorized,* and the George Polk Award for his investigative journalism.

MY FATHER DIED WHEN I WAS FOUR, my mother worked, and I was an only child with time on my hands in a poor neighborhood in the Bedford-Stuyvesant section of Brooklyn. My first two real mentors were journalists I only got to know much later in life. But I considered journalist Murray Kempton and Jimmy Cannon, a great *New York Post* sports columnist, my first mentors. Kempton made me want to read books, explore ideas, and discover irony and understatement, and reading Cannon I learned about the drama of sports and putting emotion into daily journalism. I read these two gentlemen everyday when I was in high school; reading them made me want to become a journalist.

The person who became more of a personal mentor was Michael Harrington, the author of *The Other America,* the book that inspired President Kennedy's war on poverty. In 1961, he and I got arrested together in a civil rights sit-in. Mike spent the night in a holding cell talking to four of us about the ideas of justice and equality. It was the most meaningful lecture I ever heard. Mike had come out of the Catholic Worker Movement, wanted to be a poet, and had become a radical organizer. That jailhouse sermon, quoting Dorothy Day and Martin Luther King Jr., was a vivid experience that inspired me for years to come.

Mike provided a tremendous lift to my self-esteem. He let me, a twenty-two-year-old kid with no life experience, hang out with him at the White Horse Tavern with Norman Mailer and James Baldwin. He got me my first writing assignment, with *Commonweal* magazine. He gave me confidence and inspired me to fall in love with the ideal of social justice, and the importance of direct action to improve the world.

Since I was fatherless, his impact was tremendous. My mother was not an intellectual at all, but was totally supportive of my association with Harrington, and my involvement in the civil rights movement as an activist and traveler to Mississippi.

The combination of becoming Harrington's apprentice—and reading Cannon and Kempton religiously—is what I felt made me a writer. The only way to learn journalism is by doing it, and by reading and studying good writing. And these three mentors motivated me in this direction during my formative years.

I would say that one turning point in my life was getting the job on the *Village Voice* in 1964. It was Harrington who made it happen by acting on my behalf and talking to the editor of the *Village Voice,* Dan Wolf. By then I had been the managing editor of a small radical paper called *New America,* of which Harrington was the editor. Mike had also read several of my early contributions to *Commonweal* and improved them with his editing for both style and intellectual content and reasoning.

If I learned anything from my mentors it is this: work hard. There are no shortcuts. You must have a passion for what you do. And if you work hard and have passion, then confidence will flow out of doing the thing. Showing up and doing the thing is 75 percent of the struggle.

Jessye Norman

DAVID SEIDNER

Jessye Norman has long been acknowledged as having one of the world's most beautiful voices. She has been cited for her innovative programming and fervent advocacy of contemporary music and earned recognition in the *New York Times* as "one of those once-in-a-generation singers who isn't simply following in the footsteps of others, but is staking out her own niche in the history of singing."

Ms. Norman also serves on the boards of directors for the New York Public Library, the New York Botanical Garden, Citymeals-on-Wheels in New York City, the Dance Theatre of Harlem, the National Music Foundation, and the Elton John AIDS Foundation. She is a board member as well as national spokesperson for the LUPUS Foundation and the Partnership for the Homeless. In her hometown of Augusta, Georgia, she serves on the board of trustees of Paine College and the Augusta Opera Association. An enthusiastic Girl Scout cookie seller, she is a lifetime member of the Girl Scouts.

I FEEL VERY FORTUNATE that I can think of many adults in my childhood who were influential and caring, and who offered counsel and support. My public school teachers figure prominently in this group, particularly my second-grade teacher, who invited me to sing before the entire student body when she noticed my enthusiasm for music. Of course I was thrilled. It was a large school with hundreds of students, and I felt very proud since my parents attended the school program where I sang. I was a heroine for a day—in my own classroom. It is still a wonderful memory. I feel a certain degree of confidence was acquired quite painlessly and naturally.

Other important influences came from the adults in my community and church. It was an era when adults did not hesitate to correct the behavior of children not their own because they felt the parents would agree with them completely.

As my mentors changed with my own maturation, I cannot point to just one person and say that this individual affected my life in a major way. My high school chemistry teacher propelled my interest in science and medicine, which remains with me. My junior high school music teacher made sure that I continued voice studies. She played piano for me all over my hometown of Augusta, Georgia, and many other places in the area. And, we learned songs together. She remained a valued friend.

All of my mentors were equally important. The love and care that came from growing up in a small community enabled me to find them everywhere and in many different situations. Every kind word and every act of support reminds me that I was very lucky and that it is my responsibility to express the care that I received.

L. JAY OLIVA

Dr. L. Jay Oliva was inaugurated as the fourteenth president of New York University (NYU) in 1991, the first faculty member in the history of the administration to be elevated to this position. His vision has proved to be crucial to the long-term growth and development of the university community.

Dr. Oliva earned a B.A. from Manhattan College and an M.A. and Ph.D. from Syracuse University. His fields of academic specialization are eighteenth-century Russia, Russian diplomatic theory, and eighteenth-century Europe.

Dr. Oliva has been internationally recognized for his vision of education, with honorary degrees from Tel Aviv University; University College, Dublin; Hebrew Union Collge, and Manhattan College. He also received the French Legion of Honor.

THE ROAD THAT I TRAVELED from St. Patrick's High School in Newburgh, New York, to NYU, the largest private university in the world, is one that was lined with wondrous people—those who convinced me that I could make such a journey. They refused to be put off by such problems as lack of money, or the fact that I hadn't the confidence to believe I could undertake it.

There was one person in high school who always told me that I could do anything I wanted and ultimately convinced me that it was true—Brother Basil Leo. He also taught me about the forces of continuity in life. He was relentless when he insisted that I do my best at St. Patrick's (he was also my track coach). When I moved on to Manhattan College, I found out that the brothers had transferred him ahead of me. As I got off the bus, there was Brother Basil Leo. And he was still telling me to get moving, physically and intellectually, and had no patience with reluctance.

I had two mentors in college. Brother Casimir Gabriel taught Greek and Roman history in my freshman year. I looked at this person and I listened to what he had to say, and I told myself: "Whatever it is he does, I'm going to do that." And I never gave up that dream. I decided I was going to be a professor from the start. Can you believe it? I didn't know exactly what I would profess, but I knew that this was going to be my world. Brother Gabriel taught the Renaissance and the Reformation, and I took that; and he taught the French Revolution, and I took that. In truth, I didn't really care what he taught. It was in his presence, his intellect, and his sharing nature that taught me more than all the books in the library. The second mentor was Brother Gregory, first the dean and then the president of Manhattan. In the dark of the evening I would wander into his office, where he worked late into the night, and he would put everything aside to talk about anything and everything. He made me feel important, and able to go wherever I dreamed.

So the mentoring mode has everything to do with convincing people that they can do whatever it is they want to do, and then inspiring them to make choices and see them through. This means that in mentoring you are involved not just in the delivery of information but in the creation of a life. And the concept of mentoring is incredibly important at all stages of a person's development. The capacity that college students have to encourage and support youngsters is enormous. For that reason, we established the president's C-Team at NYU, an organization of student volunteers now going into its eleventh year. The C-Team is made up of hundreds of students working as tutors and mentors for young people in Greenwich Village and the Lower East Side. The team now works with eight settlement houses and social service agencies within their preschool, after-school, and youth initiatives. Indeed, the concept of service lies at the heart of the New York University experience of our students, faculty, and staff. And in my own quiet times, I like to think that the chain of being fostered by Brother Leo, Brother Gabriel, and then Brother Gregory goes marching down through the years.

Tony Randall

Tony Randall, a renowned actor, was recently inducted into the prestigious Theatre Hall of Fame. The Emmy Award-winning actor is also an authority on opera and a serious student of the theater and art. Still noted is the successful five-year run of *The Odd Couple,* now in syndication, which was based on the play by Neil Simon.

In 1991, Randall achieved his dream with the launching of his New York City–based National Actors Theatre, a not-for-profit subscription-based company formed to bring the great classical repertoire of the world, with the finest actors, to a theater that is available to all. Randall is not only the artistic director of the company, but actor and director as well.

He lends his support and prestige to all manner of causes in which he believes. He is spokesperson for Mentoring USA and, for over two decades, has been the national chairman of the Myasthenia Gravis Foundation.

WHEN I WAS BEGINNING MY CAREER, my mentor was Charles Warburton, an old-time actor who had performed with such notable people as Ellen Terry, and who had seen Sir Henry Irving perform. He was a mine of recollections. I loved listening to his stories about all the people he had known and the great actors he had seen. During the last twenty-five years of his life, he directed a radio show called *My True Story,* and he frequently gave me roles. They didn't pay well, but they paid the rent.

One day, he asked me to stay after rehearsal and said, "I don't know what you want to do with your life, but you have something to offer this business." Those words really struck a chord in me, because his outlook on acting was different from any I had heard before. He didn't talk about success and he didn't tell me that acting was something I should do for myself. Instead, he presented it as something I could do for others. He will always have a place in my heart for showing me this way of thinking, for making acting something that was larger than me, something important to all people.

The man who taught me how to act was Sanford Meisner. He served as a mentor because he became the father-figure in my life. I received very little emotional support from my own family, so his guidance was crucial. I studied with him for two years, and he really helped me learn the business.

Both of these men played key roles in my life, not only because they were mentors to me as an actor, but because they taught me lessons about life.

KEN REGAN/CAMERA 5 © 1996

Christopher Reeve

Christopher Reeve has distinguished himself in a variety of roles on stage, screen, and television. After graduating from Cornell University, he attended Juilliard under the legendary John Houseman and made his Broadway debut with Katharine Hepburn in *A Matter of Gravity*. The success of *Superman* in 1978 and its subsequent sequels not only established Reeve's reputation as both a romantic and comic actor, but gave him the opportunity to find diverse roles in film.

Since his accident in an equestrian competition in May 1995 he has been active in raising public awareness about spinal cord injury and in obtaining increased funding from both the public and private sectors to effect a cure. The Christopher Reeve Foundation was started in January 1996 with Christopher and his wife, Dana, respectively, as president and vice president. The foundation raises funds for research for effective treatments; helps fund local and regional agencies which serve the disabled; and serves as a source of information and advocacy for disabled persons.

WHEN I THINK BACK TO MY CHILDHOOD, I don't recall any single individual who shaped my future. Instead, I benefited from the influence of a number of adults, in my family, at school, and in the theater.

My parents separated when I was not quite four years old, and when I was six my mother remarried. My stepfather was a successful stockbroker who already had four children from a previous marriage, but he was more than willing to take on the responsibility of the two young boys who came along with his new wife. My father, an academic, had also remarried and soon had three more children with my stepmother. I spent much of my childhood shuttling back and forth between the two families.

The two households could not possibly have been more different. In my father's house there were always writers and musicians. By the time I was seven I had asked my mother for piano lessons, which I continued to take through my freshman year at college.

My father was also very athletic. In the winters he took his family skiing in Vermont, and in the summers we all crowded aboard his twenty-two-foot sailboat. Because my father made these activities so enjoyable they became an important part of my life, lasting all the way into adulthood.

But there was one difficult aspect of the time I spent with my father: he was a perfectionist who was often intolerant of even simple mistakes. I put intense pressure on myself to avoid his disapproval. Even though I often failed, I think I learned a valuable lesson, which I have tried to keep in mind in bringing up my own children: challenge them, but never set them up for failure.

The atmosphere in my other family was quite chaotic by comparison. My stepfather had to work long hours, even on weekends, to meet all his financial obligations. But he was tremendously generous. His philosophy seemed to be: provide children with opportunities and let them learn by trial and error. As long as each child behaved responsibly, he was a cheerleader on the sidelines. When one of his eight young charges ran into difficulty, he stepped in and became a coach.

I was given a tremendous amount of freedom at a young age, and became fascinated with the theater. Soon I was playing leads in plays at school as well as working backstage, and eventually onstage, with the highly regarded McCarter Theatre Repertory Company.

At the McCarter Theatre I had my first formal experience of mentoring. The artistic director was Arthur Lithgow, father of the actor John Lithgow. During one performance, I was horsing around backstage when I found myself face-to-face with Arthur. I remember him chastising me for playing such an immature game instead of preparing for my entrance. But then he said something I will never forget: "You may be the one in a thousand who succeeds in the theater. You'd better decide what you want, because you'll probably get it." In an instant I realized that it is a privilege to appear onstage and that while it may be fun to fool around occasionally, fun is nothing compared to the satisfaction of doing something well. I believe my entire approach to being an actor was formed at that moment.

I also believe that my successes have resulted primarily from this unusual combination of early influences. I had learned independence, but also self-discipline. I'm not sure that either my father or stepfather realized the profound effect that each had on my development. They were mentors without even knowing it. Later in life I would come in contact with excellent teachers and fellows who inspired me with their talent. It is only because I was given so much freedom and so many privileges as a child that I was able to make the most of the opportunities that were to come my way.

LEONARD RIGGIO

Leonard Riggio is the founder, chairman, and chief executive officer of Barnes and Noble, Inc., the parent company of Barnes and Noble Bookstores, barnesandnoble.com, B. Dalton Booksellers, and Doubleday Book Shops.

A native New Yorker, Mr. Riggio began his career in bookselling in 1958 when he went to work in the New York University bookstore while attending college at night. In 1965 he opened his first bookstore, called the SBX, in Greenwich Village, serving local college students.

He serves on the boards of the Brooklyn Tech Foundation, the Children's Defense Fund, and Poets and Writers, and is vice chairman of the Fifth Avenue Association. He has been a guest lecturer at many universities, delivered commencement addresses, and been keynote speaker to numerous educational and business groups across the country.

I AM FORTUNATE TO HAVE HAD THREE great mentors, each of whom have had a profound impact on my life: my father, Steve Riggio; my coworker and friend, Hamilton Dolly; and my first and only boss, Al Zavelle.

Steve Riggio was one of seven children who grew up in a tightly knit Italian-American family in Little Italy in Manhattan. He was a brilliant man and a great athlete. Eventually, he became a highly ranked prizefighter, whose claim to fame was that he twice defeated Rocky Graziano, who had never been beaten twice before.

Dad did not like to lose anymore than he liked to get hit. After eighty-five professional fights, he left the ring without a scar on his face, and unlike most prizefighters, he never slurred his words. He remained handsome and brilliantly articulate for the rest of his life. He viewed boxing as both a science and an art, studying and practicing like no one else in the game. He won because he outboxed and outtrained his opponents. The power of his will was amazing.

Dad was completely focused on the relationship between mind and body, believing that the health of one would improve the health of the other. He drew his strength from his brain, and nourished his mind from the underpinnings of a sound body. Even later, when he became a cab driver, he would always work out. At traffic lights, he would get out of the cab and do deep-knee bends and push-ups. Other cabbies thought he was crazy, but they never told him to his face.

I played a lot of sports growing up, and was usually the best kid on the block or on the team at most things I played. Much of this was due to the countless hours I spent at practice and the hustle I brought to the game. To this extent, I was a model for dad's beliefs: I was dedicated, focused, and relentless.

Surprisingly for a boxer, dad believed in weight training for most sports. He was thirty years ahead of his time in thinking that basketball players and golfers should lift weights. Back in the early 1950s, he also preached to my grandmother about working out. He was convinced that senior citizens could extend their life expectancy and add to their self-esteem with a simple fitness routine. To this extent, he was the consummate optimist. His enthusiasm and energy inspired everyone he met.

Steve Riggio also believed that a sound and active mind needed work and practice. He worked his mind as hard as he did his body. He never felt that people were born smarter than he was, and he easily made up for environmental deficiencies through his lifelong curiosity and intuition. Although dad never graduated from high school, he completed the *New York Times* crossword puzzle nearly every day. "The pen is mightier than the sword," he would say. "Wars are nothing more than the battles over different ideas."

But, to him, mentoring was not making his children into clones of himself. He gave me the resolve to live by the courage of my own convictions, not his beliefs. He rarely tried to rein me in, preferring to let me develop my own set of values and navigation system. The only thing he ever offered, which was close to an admonition, was this: "There is nothing in this world you can't do, and nothing in this universe you can't become, if you put your mind to it." He would also qualify this advice a bit and say, "Hitch your wagon to a star and you'll never land short of the moon." For those who later described me as having "humble beginnings," they never met my dad and mentor, Steve Riggio.

High aspirations and indomitable will were also the attributes of my mentor, friend, and coworker, Hamilton Dolly. More than any other person before or since, Hamilton opened my eyes to the bigger world around me, purging forever my provincial inclinations, and encouraging, even exhorting, me to fulfill my own destiny.

Growing up in Brooklyn during the McCarthy era, I was colored with ignorant misconceptions and outright paranoia. Just years removed from the greatest atrocities in the history of the world, the fires of prejudice burned ever brightly in America. Union activists were considered Communists; Jews were viewed with suspicion and distrust; and African Americans were treated as second-class citizens. Although dad was a brilliant and compassionate man, his own worldview was shaped by his limited exposure; he could not, alone, expose me to the next level I so sorely needed.

Working alongside Hamilton Dolly at the New York University bookstore, I was literally bombarded with conflicting and hopelessly complex points of view. Nothing in my past provided context for the issues I needed to resolve. During these formative years, Hamilton was my mentor and my beacon. He was, without a doubt, the most brilliant person I ever encountered. He mind was as fit, as hard, and as facile as dad's considerable physique.

As the manager of the textbook department, Hamilton took it upon himself to conduct a character-building school for the young people he supervised. He believed, as dad did, that indefatigable effort could overcome environmental shortcomings. He lived and taught by what for him was a necessary principle: "It's *not* who you know, but *what* you know and what you *do* which creates success." He thought people should be connected to themselves before worrying about "connecting" to other people.

Hamilton always did, and continues to, believe that good work is its own reward. He instilled pride and dignity and purpose in hundreds of people, largely from minority groups, that he trained. He was a role model in providing an example of how to act, but he was a brilliant mentor in teaching people how to think.

The NYU bookstore also provided me with Al Zavelle, my first and only boss. "Mr. Zavelle" was the very first symbol of authority that I encountered in the real world outside of my home, but, fortunately for me, he represented the high-mindedness necessary to be a great leader. He taught me what he knew by example and explanation. To this day, he continues to write me useful notes and kind words of encouragement. To him, mentoring is clearly a lifetime commitment.

Understanding the importance of rationalizing the intersections between responsibility and authority, he took the work of managing a bookstore most seriously. In fact, he was the first college bookstore manager in America to whom the title of director was conferred, because he made the business of selling textbooks to college students an all-encompassing mission. Not satisfied with being just another administrator, he considered himself part of the faculty, and his role as critical in the process of education. To him I owe the concept of bringing missionary zeal to the workplace.

Over the course of his life, Al Zavelle always broke the mold, because he was never satisfied with the status quo. Back in the days when computers were a primitive technology, he oversaw the complete automation of the NYU bookstore's elaborate inventory management system, a feat which would not be duplicated for five years after we were up and running. A study in self-improvement, he earned his M.B.A. in night school while working as bookstore director during the day. Naturally, he was a straight-A student, because the man simply would not accept mediocrity in anything he ever attempted.

On one occasion, as Mr. Zavelle was conducting a tour of the school supply section I managed, he came to a spot on the shelves where a certain brand of typing paper used to sit.

"What's that?" he said.

"That's the 409-IP," I replied. "It's on order."

At this point, he pointed to the empty space angrily and said, "I don't give a damn about what is on order. Our students can't type their homework on your excuses."

Although this stinging retribution spoiled my otherwise pleasant day, I have prospered since by remembering its message: excuses are often the fine line between successful people and those who are victims of their own lack of resolve.

To this day, our college bookstore company, which now consists of more than three hundred stores, operates under this single admonition, thanks to the genius of Al Zavelle: "Cover thy shelves."

Steve Riggio, Hamilton Dolly, and Al Zavelle were three historic figures in my life, and three great mentors. My life was clearly nourished by what they contributed, and their lives were to some extent enriched by what I have achieved. Mentoring is all about the nurturing relationship between mentor and the mentored: each growing because of the other. Although there can be a profound difference between mentors and heroes, some individuals embody the greatness of both.

NBC NEWS

GERALDO RIVERA

Geraldo Rivera—hard-hitting investigative reporter, accomplished interviewer, and champion of citizens' rights—is one of America's most successful television journalists and public advocates. Through his distinguished work as an author, news producer, talk show host, and philanthropist, Rivera has made enormous contributions in the fields of broadcasting and community service.

Since the start of his news career, Rivera has covered seven wars, conducted exclusive interviews with the likes of Fidel Castro and Charles Manson, authored more than five books, and received more than 170 awards for his work in television journalism. These honors include the prestigious George Foster Peabody Award, three national and seven local Emmys, and two Robert F. Kennedy, Columbia-DuPont, and Scripps Howard Journalism Awards. He has also received three honorary doctorate degrees.

Rivera, who loves to sail, hopes to cross the international dateline at the turn of the century on his seventy-foot ketch, *Voyager.*

I LIKE TO SAY THAT MY LIFE has had more ups and downs than the Cyclone roller coaster at Coney Island. In terms of my professional life, probably the most profound turning point was the decision to leave the law and pursue a career in journalism. I had worked so hard to become a lawyer that to leave the law, switch professions, and attend Columbia University seemed a step backward to most of my friends and family.

The lessons I learned in the early stage of coming of age mostly revolved around the importance of education—staying in school, getting equipped for the world beyond. Education in America is a great equalizer, the way to level the field so that each could be judged on his or her own abilities. Once I was out of high school and in college, my options were much larger than those available to either of my parents.

There are four men I consider my mentor heroes.

Russell Van Brunt, my high school principal, helped me not to succumb to the temptations of the street or the quick independence of blue-collar life. Because of him, I decided on a college career that led to everything else of importance in my life.

Julius C. C. Edelstein, a former advisor to Mayor Robert Wagner and later an official at the City University of New York, taught me how to moderate my ethnic and ideological anger and channel it into positive energy directed toward responsible social change.

Fred Friendly, the giant of broadcasting, became my teacher and guide at the Columbia School of Journalism. He was the champion of integration of the news business. He urged me to be myself, not to try to mimic others. He also urged me to use my life experience to bring a different perspective to the screen.

Roone Arledge, another broadcasting giant, ignored the rap against me by many mainstream journalists and gave me the opportunity to prove myself on a brand new program called *20/20.*

What made these four mentors so important to my life and career was their steadfast loyalty and their patience, despite the many times that I disappointed them. Fred Friendly, for example, was my principle cheerleader in the network news business. He told me that if I wanted to make the world a better place through the law, then I would have vastly more opportunities to do that in broadcast journalism. He was right.

In my high school days, I was a confused and insecure young man. No one in my very large family—my father was one of twenty-one children, my mother one of eight—had ever been to college. What these men did for me was open my mind to possibilities that existed beyond the narrow confines of the world I knew. They told me I was smart, that I had potential, and that the world, while potentially hostile, was still a place that rewarded hard work and big dreams. Later they taught me the importance of sticking with my instincts, not conforming for the sake of being like the other guy. And to make sure that my positions were based on research and data, not attitude or prejudice.

LEANDRO P. RIZZUTO

Leandro P. Rizzuto, chairman, president, and owner of the Conair Corporation, founded Conair in 1959 with his parents, Julian and Josephine, and a $100 investment. In 1959, Conair revolutionized the industry with the invention of the wire hair roller, and in 1971 perfected the first pistol-grip hair dryer. Conair's impact on the professional beauty industry has earned Rizzuto recognition, including Sears's prestigious Partners in Progress award for excellence in manufacturing consumer appliances; Eckerd Corporation's Vendor Appreciation award; the SPARC (Supplier Performance Award by Retail Category) award for nine years as the nation's number-one supplier in the personal care appliance category; and the K Mart award of recognition for exceptional achievement.

IT IS TOUGH NOT TO MENTION my mom and dad as the principle influences in my life. I attribute a tremendous amount of success to their guidance and input in both business and personal areas.

My mom and dad were Italian immigrants, both hairdressers. As a kid, my dad learned that hard work and long hours were the keys to success, and that in America, anything was possible. He also believed that your mind was limited by your imagination. Being a hairdresser, he decided to create products based on the needs of a salon. Being in America, he had the ability to capitalize on his ideas.

Conair started as a family business in 1959 with an initial investment of $100. Today, sales exceed $800 million. But when the business started back in 1959, it was Mom, Dad, and me in the basement of our house. Dad not only invented hair rollers, but took charge of their manufacture, production, and distribution. He went from bobby pins to pin clips to hair rollers, and in 1970 he perfected the hair dryer. Each step of the way, his inventions were responsible for the next evolution of services and products for hair salons.

Where Dad was creative, Mom was more business-oriented and managed beauty salons. She knew about the books, the expenses, the importance of organization, and making profits. With her guidance I learned about expansion and comprehensive marketing, things which, taken together, help a business succeed. I wouldn't be where I am today without the skills she taught me.

Luckily I am a mixture of both my parents. They showed that sacrifice was a key to success. If you work hard, it will pay off. And it has.

Outside of my family, John Kluge has been a great mentor. He also believed in the value of hard work. He arrived in America from Holland at age nine, and eventually received a scholarship to Columbia University. After graduating he entered the military service and then the business world, becoming very successful in media activities.

I've always sought his advice in business and personal matters.

He has acted as my sounding board since the mid-1970s in advertising, international activities, acquisitions, or other financial opportunities for the company. Through his example, John taught me that we should give back to those who have helped us, whether they are people or institutions. He has been a strong supporter and a main financial contributor to Columbia University. He feels the school took a chance in giving him a scholarship, and now he wants others to have the same opportunities that he was given. Today, in his "young" eighties, he is still active, still a pioneer in his field, and one of the most successful businessmen in America.

John Kluge taught me to give back to my community, and my parents taught me the value of family, especially in the context of a family-run business. My four children are all involved in Conair, and like my parents before me, I'm trying to pass on to them my own experience and know-how. I hope this will aid them in their own lives. I know it helped in mine.

© 1994 BIG HELP—TOM QUEALLY

Herb Scannell

Herb Scannel is the president of Nickelodeon/Nick at Nite/Nick at Nite's TV Land. As president he is responsible for all creative and business operations. He has successfully led Nickelodeon's continuing innovations in original TV productions, programming for kids and families, international channels and program blocks, movies, licensed products, publishing, recreation, and public affairs.

In the fall of 1996, under Scannell's guidance, Nickelodeon used its position as the number-one network in cable television to expand into original animation and feature films and prime time. Mr. Scannell has also overseen the network's repositioning of the Nick Jr. preschool programming block.

Scannell was instrumental in creating Nick at Nite's TV

Land, a twenty-four-hour network based on classic television. It has proven to be one of basic cable's most successful new networks in years. Now seen in over twenty-one million homes, TV Land blends the best shows from over forty years of television.

BESIDES MY PARENTS, there were three individuals who served as influential mentors for me over the course of my life and career. The first person was my brother Ray. He was the oldest of four children, and six years older than me. My dad wasn't really into sports, but my brother was key to my social development because he taught me to play sports, especially baseball. Sports helped me to socialize with other kids.

It was my brother who also first introduced me to pop culture through music; through him I discovered rock and roll. He also provided a world view of the turbulent 1960s and early '70s. A political activist, he showed me ways of questioning the status quo that stay with me today.

Following in my brother's footsteps, I went to Boston College. While my brother was interested in student government, I got involved in radio. Through radio, I could continue to be part of what I loved—entertainment, pop culture, and, most importantly, music. After I graduated, I wanted to stay in radio. One of my sister's friends had a brother, Fred Seibert, who worked for a radio station. He turned out to be another influential person in my life.

Fred somehow helped me get a job at a country music radio station as an assistant to the director of marketing and promotions. Two weeks later, my boss quit. Here I was at twenty-two, not knowing anything about country music, not even really liking country music, and I'm supposed to be the head of marketing and promotions! I didn't know what I was doing and—I was terrified. Luckily for me there was Fred. I could call him anytime and he was more than willing to help me out.

On a more profound level, Fred made me a better thinker. He reminded me of my brother in that he always stressed the importance of questioning the way things were and looking at change as a positive possibility.

Fred is still in my life and I'm still asking him questions. And, I'm not alone. He's mentor to a lot of people in the company and still challenges people to be better thinkers in the workplace and the world.

The third mentor in my life will always be very special to me. Her name is Gerry Laybourne. When I started at Nickelodeon, she was president. Gerry was an inspiration in the workplace. She wanted to see people collaborate and work together, and she believed that the best kind of management was collaborative "team management" versus a hierarchical approach. She practiced what she preached. Her door was always open and available to me to discuss problems and help me arrive at solutions alone or with my peers. When she left Nickelodeon, I got the chance to run the company, and lead, as her mentoring has inspired me to do.

I've been extremely fortunate in life. The people I've grown up with, have met, and been associated with have made my life full. I feel very lucky.

José E. Serrano

Congressman Serrano was born in Mayaguez, Puerto Rico, in 1942. In 1950, his family moved to the South Bronx, where he attended public schools. He served in the 172nd Support Battalion, in the U.S. Army Medical Corps, at Fort Wainright, Alaska.

José E. Serrano is currently serving his fifth consecutive term in the U.S. House of Representatives, where he represents the newly drawn Sixteenth Congressional District in the South Bronx, New York City. The first bill for which Serrano was prime sponsor was signed into law in 1990, providing funding for successful school dropout prevention programs. He has cosponsored a number of major bills, including the Civil Rights Act, the Family and Medical Leave Act, the Higher Education Act, the Brady gun control bill, and the Cesar Chavez Workplace Fairness Act. Prior to his election to Congress in 1990, Mr. Serrano had a distinguished career in the New York State Assembly, including six years as chairman of the education committee.

WHEN I WAS YOUNGER, I was very interested in becoming an actor, and when I was about fifteen or sixteen, I came across a tiny theater program in the South Bronx. It was run by two men, Salvatore Gulla and Frederick Halaman Daris. I was a young Puerto Rican, while Fred and Sal were both white. Despite our differences, and despite all the racial stereotypes I had been exposed to, these two people really became mentors for me.

Over the years I have kept in touch with Fred, who, through his advice and especially his example, became a person I always felt I could turn to for support. He never preached, but would comment on people and their behavior. I listened and learned from him.

During the late 1960s, when there was constant confrontation in the street—antiwar demonstrations, the rise of the Black Panthers, increased racial tension—Fred was an incredible influence on me. He had respect and love for all minority groups, and a strong commitment to children. From him, I learned the importance of respect for all people, and sacrifice for those who were less fortunate than myself.

In 1969, I took a job as a school paraprofessional. During the five years I worked with Fred, he sent me out into the community to talk about the theater program. This assignment allowed me to meet the people in the neighborhood, which gave me the support I needed to run for the state assembly. They urged me to run, and Fred offered his heartfelt support. I can honestly say that the opportunities he gave me in the community played a major role in my election to the state assembly, and later to Congress.

We live in a society where people get credit for what they do, and rightly so. But many of the people who have influenced successful, recognized individuals go unnoticed. Nobody writes about Fred Daris, but he is part of the reason people write about me. Because of him, I can never be indifferent to the needs of children and teenagers, and I have based my politics on what he taught me. More than an adviser, more than a teacher, he has been an example to me, and has shown me the importance of love, respect, and self-sacrifice—values that should be a part of everyone's life.

DARIO ACOSTA

MARTIN SHEEN

The prolific career of Martin Sheen (Ramon Estevez) has stretched from stage to screen to television. Born the seventh child of ten to a Spanish immigrant father and an Irish mother, Sheen first won critic's notice on Broadway at the age of twenty-four when he played the lead in *The Subject Was Roses.* Some of his unforgettable roles in film have been in Terence Malick's *Badlands* and Francis Ford Coppola's *Apocalypse Now.*

Sheen is active in the antinuclear campaign and has been arrested several times during protests. He is a national spokesperson for Mentoring USA and has appeared in a public service announcement promoting the project.

"When the student is ready the teacher will appear" is an old cliché that was certainly fulfilled in my life by three very different mentors who seemed to materialize at the most opportune times when I was young and most receptive. Although they could not have been more diverse in personality and background, they could not have been more alike at the core of their character or the depth of their humanity.

All three were white males—two were middle class, one was very poor—and each of their young lives had been profoundly formed by the Great Depression of the 1930s. Two were Jewish from the urban East and one was Roman Catholic from the Midwest. Despite great family hardships and personal tragedy early on, none of them confronted life as a problem to be solved; on the contrary, each had accepted his life as a wonderful and mysterious gift to be cherished and explored. Along with varying levels of education and an abundance of natural social skills, each had developed a disciplined commitment to personal growth and service to others, and, equally important, each had a unique sense of humor. Above all, as if by design, each one seemed to have developed his own deeply personal spirituality which revealed itself in compassion.

In order of appearance in my life they were: Rev. Alfred Drapp, assistant pastor at Holy Trinity Parish and School in Dayton, Ohio; Julian Beck, cofounder and director of the Living Theater in New York, and Joseph Papp, the founder and director of the New York Shakespeare Festival and the New York Public Theatre.

Father Al arrived at Holy Trinity for his first parish assignment when I was fourteen. He was an energetic young man with an innate wisdom who believed our personal relationships were reflective of our relationship to God. It was not long before he was having a noticeable effect on every family in the parish despite his lifelong struggle with shyness, which endeared him to us all the more. I served mass for him regularly, and he was my confessor.

Even as a boy I dreamed of going to New York after high school to pursue an acting career, but my father was determined that I attend college. A deformed left shoulder at birth made me, in my father's eyes, incapable of earning a living as a laborer. Hence the necessity of a higher education. This became the most contentious issue between us for a number of years. Unfortunately, I was never a good student, and when I flunked out of high school in my senior year my father was disappointed and angry. Father Al advised me to go to summer school and graduate. He also suggested that to appease my father I agree to take the entrance exams to the University of Dayton. I did both.

Unknown to anyone, I purposely failed the exam, scoring just 3 percent out of a possible 100. My father got the message, but still would not bless my dream. Perhaps he wanted to see some proof of my talent or determination. Father Al stepped forward again and, careful not to offend my father, he loaned me enough money, out of his own pocket, to get started and soon I was on my way. Several months later, when I was settled in New York building a life for myself in the theater, my father very lovingly came around and became my biggest supporter.

Over the years my relationship with Father Al matured and his friendship became invaluable. Although my journey took me far away and at times I became lost, he was always there like an anchor reminding me to continually ask those two key little questions: Who are you? Why are you here? As long as I can answer at least one of them I always know where I'm going, and Father Al will always remain with me.

I began working at the Living Theatre in December 1959, and for the next two-and-a-half years my formation as an actor and a human being were greatly enhanced under the tutelage of Julian Beck, cofounder of this remarkable avant-garde and politically active repertory company at 14th Street and 6th Avenue in New York City.

It was here that I made my professional acting debut, my first trip to Europe (in the summer of 1961, when the company represented the United States in the Theatre of Nations Festival in Paris, and won the Grand Prix), and it was here where I met my future wife, Janet Templeton. It was at the Living Theatre that I made personal contact with Dorothy Day's Catholic worker movement, which remains to this day a powerful source of grace in my life.

And it was here that my talent was realized and flourished, and my career began in earnest. It was also here that I was exposed to nonviolence as a practical way of life.

Julian Beck was thirty-six when I met him, and although he was six feet, two inches, he never weighed more than 150 pounds in his adult life. This, coupled with his early loss of hair and unusually pale complexion, gave him a much older and extremely frail appearance despite his great energy.

One night as I was sweeping the stairway between floors at the theater a very large and unruly character appeared, demanding to see one of the actors who was on stage at the time. Julian was summoned, and he politely pleaded with the man to leave a message for the actor and depart, since he was causing such a disturbance. But the man refused and became even more unruly, cursing Julian and making violent threats. Julian continued in a firm but compassionate manner to dissuade him when suddenly this fellow reared back and slapped Julian across the face with a blow that sent him flying backward down the stairs and into my arms. I was terrified, knowing full well that this madman could destroy both of us with ease, but before I could respond, Julian righted himself, took a deep breath, and then very calmly walked back up to the man and again in the same, compassionate manner asked him to leave.

The man was so completely disarmed and shamed that he simply looked away and muttered some unintelligible curse as he brushed past us, going back down the stairs and out the door. In that instant the personal cost of nonviolence was made as clear to me as the blood red imprint of the man's hand on the side of Julian's face. Each time I face arrest during nonviolent civil disobedience actions for peace and social justice, I remember how extraordinary and ironic that such a frail man could teach such a powerful and lifelong lesson. I was nineteen years old then, and I had never seen such an astonishing nonviolent response to such an aggressive act. And I had been raised a Catholic in the faith of the nonviolent Jesus.

One day in 1963 I gave a very energetic audition for a New York Shakespeare Festival public high school touring company production of *Macbeth*. The director was sufficiently impressed to offer me a small role for very little money, which I politely and promptly rejected, since I was married with a growing family to support. In retrospect, I should have eagerly accepted the role despite the hardship it promised, since it would have united me with theater icon and future mentor Joseph Papp much earlier. This handsome, complex, delightfully pugnacious, disarmingly humorous, deeply compassionate, enviably courageous, self-educated, Brooklyn-born Shakespearean scholar was arguably the single most influential force on the American theatre in this century. Like everyone who loved him, I called him Joe, and he was the only man, other than my father, who called me Ramon, my real name.

I worked with Joe many times over the years in productions of *Antony and Cleopatra, Hamlet,* and *Julius Caesar.* But the one I chiefly loved was *Romeo and Juliet* in which Joe directed and I played Romeo in the summer of 1968 for Central Park. A few days into rehearsal we were working on the famous so-called Queen Mab scene, where Mercutio first appears with dazzling speeches and overwhelming energy. It suddenly occurred to me that I was playing the wrong part. I should have been playing Mercutio, and not Romeo. I concocted a scenario which I presented to Joe after rehearsal in the hope that he would see the wisdom of my decision and make the switch.

Ever careful not to offend the great Shakespearean maestro for a casting error, and quick to express my deep gratitude for his boundless faith in trusting me with the title role, I pleaded my case for the role of Mercutio with passion. "Let's face it, Joe," I said. "I am not a lovesick and dull Romeo type, rather, an energetic and heroic Mercutio type." On and on I went, from the time it took us to walk from the rehearsal hall up three flights of stairs and across the lobby to his office. Along the way Joe listened patiently, never interrupting my diatribe as he unwrapped and prepared a fresh cigar.

As I concluded my argument he looked me in the eye and without hesitation said, "Of course you could play Mercutio. It's not a real challenge for you. That's why you must play Romeo." As I absorbed the truthful shock of his remark, he lit the cigar and said, "Good night, Romeo. See you at rehearsal tomorrow."

It is not possible to overstate the measure of influence these three extraordinary men had on every aspect of my life. Nor can I account for my remarkably good fortune to have known and loved them anymore than I can comprehend the immeasurable conduit of grace their lives still impart to me long after their deaths. But when I was asked to be a mentor myself, my response was a foregone conclusion, thanks to three guys called Julian, Joe, and Al, and the profound effect they had on a boy named Ramon.

TIMOTHY WHITE/FOX

Andrew Shue

Actor, activist, athlete, entrepreneur. Since graduating from Dartmouth College in 1989, Andrew Shue, thirty-one, has succeeded in many fields. For the last six years, he has also starred on the hit TV show *Melrose Place,* and he recently made his film debut in *The Rainmaker.*

As a community leader, he is cofounder and chairman of the nonprofit organization Do Something, which has inspired and trained hundreds of thousands of young people to take action as responsible citizens. Over the last five years, he has been instrumental in raising over $10 million and forming strategic partnerships with MTV, Fox Television, Blockbuster Entertainment, and America Online.

As an athlete, Shue has committed twenty-five years to his first love—soccer. He has played professionally for the top team in Zimbabwe and served as a pioneer player and spokesman for the Los Angeles Galaxy and major league soccer. In 1990, he also spent a year teaching high school math in Bulawayo, Zimbabwe.

I COME FROM A SOCIALLY active family. My grandfather was a principal of a school, my grandmother was a teacher, my mom worked for the United Way, and my father ran for Congress. I remember sitting on my dad's shoulders at a rally in the early 1970s—I must have been three or four—when he was backing legislation to lower the voting age from twenty-one to eighteen. He felt that those who were old enough to be drafted and die in Vietnam should have more of a voice in the political arena.

Both my brothers were Eagle Scouts and were heavily involved in community service projects. My dad nudged me into community service, too, not saying "you must do this," but rather suggesting that it was something I might find rewarding. During my junior year in high school I started a program called Students Serving Seniors, which brought young people to rest homes. It continues to this day.

My adviser for student council, Owen Snyder, also played an important role in my life. He was an incredible teacher and became a good friend. I always remember the time he explained to me why I was a good kid. It wasn't because I was a good soccer player or school president, but because I was interesting, thoughtful, and willing to be honest about my fears. His words had a huge impact on my self-image, for they helped me believe that I was a good person inside. This was a critical lesson early on—everyone must truly value who they are on the inside rather than the outside. Mr. Snyder's influence has extended to all areas of my life. The sense of self-worth he gave me has had an impact on everything I do and every relationship I have had.

I had a soccer coach at Dartmouth, Bobby Clark, who was instrumental in my playing professional soccer in Zimbabwe. Coach Clark is a person who leads by example; he always stressed actions over words—it was more about what he did rather than what he said. This was also an important lesson for me.

In addition to playing soccer in Zimbabwe, I taught math to school kids there. I had been inspired by my parents, who had taught in Nigeria at the same age as I did when they were in a program that would later become the Peace Corps. I was simply recreating their dream experience. Working, rather than just traveling, abroad is something I would suggest to anyone. It was a great experience for me.

Life is only meaningful when shared. It is through connecting with others that we open our eyes to understanding and caring, not only with ourselves but with others as well.

MURIEL SIEBERT

Muriel "Mickie" Siebert is the founder and president of the national discount brokerage firm that bears her name, Muriel Siebert and Co., Inc. She established the firm in 1967 when she became the first woman member of the New York Stock Exchange. Today the New York City–based firm has offices in Florida, New Jersey, Texas, Michigan, Washington, and California, as well as a growing capital markets division. Muriel Siebert and Co. is the only woman-owned NYSE brokerage firm with a national presence in the United States. Ms. Siebert continues to oversee the firm's day-to-day operations.

Throughout her career, Ms. Siebert has been actively involved with a wide range of nonprofit, civic, and women's organizations.

THERE HAVE BEEN MANY PEOPLE in business who have helped me or given advice, but no one really served as a mentor to the extent of my Uncle Frank. He was a highly influential figure in my life. A remarkable man, he was very close to my mother and me at a time when both of us needed family support.

During my college years my father was in the midst of a three-year battle with cancer. We had around-the-clock nurses at our house and I was cutting classes at Case Western Reserve University and playing bridge. It was a difficult time for my mother and me, but her family really helped out during these years. My Uncle Frank (my mother's brother) and Aunt Tootsie (my mother's sister, whose real name was Sara) would come to our house and just take charge. They would get my mom and me out of the house and help ease the tension of my father's condition. We would go to the Petty Bone Club and play bingo or just go to the movies.

Uncle Frank owned a plastics factory in Cleveland, where he and his wife lived until she developed respiratory problems and couldn't breathe there. They moved to Tucson to ease her breathing problems. Uncle Frank opened another plastics factory in Tucson and continued to keep the old factory in Cleveland as well.

"Do your best and leave the rest to God," he would always say. He had a wonderfully positive attitude toward life that was inspiring, and his example helped develop the same attitude in me. He lived to be ninety-five years old, and I think he may have seen only one doctor in about sixty-five years. He was a Christian Scientist and helped with many of their charitable movements. He donated land for a Christian Science retirement home in Arizona and worked as a volunteer in their reading rooms in Tucson. He will always be the selfless man who was ready to lend a helping hand to those in need.

TABITHA SOREN

MICHAEL LAVINE

Tabitha Soren is an award-winning MTV News reporter and anchor. In 1991 she came to MTV News from the ABC affiliate in Vermont. While still in college she worked at WNBC, CNN, and on ABC's *World News Tonight,* with Peter Jennings. Then, from 1994 to 1996, she worked for NBC News as a correspondent. She has written for the *Los Angeles Times* and *USA Today,* and also wrote a bimonthly column for the *New York Times* syndicate for four years.

During her tenure at MTV, Ms. Soren has worked on a wide variety of documentary specials. She has investigated topics such as women in the military, teen pregnancy, and the sexual abuse of children, as well as reported on the 1992 and 1996 presidential campaigns. She also produces, develops, and writes the stories that she covers.

DORIS DANCY WAS MY ENGLISH TEACHER and head of the English Honor Society, of which I was president. She taught me to love prose as well as poetry, encouraging me to write my own. In the process, I reaped the emotional, spiritual, and intellectual benefits of being immersed in literature. In Ms. Dancy's classroom, writing wasn't just about getting good grades. It was about expressing myself and discovering what I thought about the world around me. Reading books was more than homework, it was a way to broaden my small-town perspective on the world.

She was also a very religious woman who presented me with a Bible as a graduation present. However, she was hardly a Bible-thumper. She said the Good Book was a way to trace the roots of all books, because the stories and lessons in the Bible serve as the framework for countless other classics. It seems obvious to me now, but no one had ever put the Bible in a literary context for me before. Ms. Dancy taught me to believe in myself at a vulnerable, awkward time, and to know that I could do anything as long as I had confidence in my abilities. The only faith she forced on me was faith in myself.

Dave Schindel was my adviser on the school newspaper as well as my journalism teacher. High school ceased to be torture around Mr. Schindel. In addition to introducing me to the basics of print journalism ethics and techniques, this easygoing former hippie helped me look on the bright side. He was always humming some ridiculous Donovan song or getting up on an amusing soapbox about President Reagan's right-wing politics. His playfulness was instrumental in preventing me from being overcome with anxieties about SAT scores, college admissions, and financial aid. He impressed on me that there were things in life one just couldn't control and that life could be unpredictable no matter how hard you worked, studied, or prepared. It was important for me to be ready for the unfair and sometimes painful experiences one is presented in life so I didn't have a meltdown when disappointment came my way. Mr. Schindel also stressed how resilient human beings were—even teenagers—and how no single test score, school, or job would make or break my happiness. He, too, taught me to believe in myself by being more confident in my future success.

Mr. Schindel and Ms. Dancy were the individuals who encouraged me to leave my friends and family behind in Virginia, where I attended Hampton High School, and head to New York City to fulfill my dreams as a journalist. They gave me the confidence and security to know that I could make an impact on the world. Under their guidance, I realized that the people who succeed are those who have the courage to take risks, who aren't paralyzed by the possibility of rejection, who decline to accept a glass ceiling, who are comfortable having unpopular opinions, and who refuse to listen to people who say, "Never."

Ms. Dancy and Mr. Schindel were my inspirations in high school, and they continue to impact my world today. I am indebted to them for what I have accomplished thus far and for helping me become who I am.

PAUL SORVINO

Veteran actor Paul Sorvino most recently appeared in Warren Beatty's *Bulworth.* He has also appeared in countless other films, including *William Shakespeare's Romeo and Juliet, Nixon, The Firm,* and *GoodFellas.*

On television, he starred in the NBC series *Law and Order* as well as *The Oldest Rookie, We'll Get By,* and *Bert D'Angelo, Superstar.* He has also appeared in many theater productions. He was the star in the Broadway production of *That Champion Season,* which earned him a 1973 New York Drama Critics Circle Award.

An accomplished tenor, Sorvino sang the role of Alfred in *Die Fledermaus* with the Seattle Opera Company. He has also performed at New York's Metropolitan Opera House and recorded three CDs.

He is the founder of the Sorvino Children's Asthma Foundation and the author of *How to Become a Former Asthmatic.* He also founded and served as the artistic director of the American Stage Company at Fairleigh Dickinson University.

In his spare time, Sorvino paints, sculpts, plays the piano, writes poetry in a form that is two-centuries old, and plays tennis.

I HAD A RAGTAG EDUCATION. No one took me under their wing or turned the tide for me—I always had to show myself the ropes. This independent streak originated with my mom. My father was a complex man who tried too hard to foster a sense of perfection, which caused me to reject his type of guidance at a fairly young age. My mother, on the other hand, took success and failure calmly, and she offered unconditional encouragement, acceptance, and love.

My mother is the individual who served as my primary influence. She made me believe that anything was possible, that I was capable of anything. Her extreme generosity was her most salient quality. She set the standard for my conception of women, whom I have always felt to be benevolent presences in my life.

She was musically gifted, an extremely talented pianist who always encouraged my interest in painting, and it remains one of my favorite artistic endeavors. Once, as a child, I drew on our front door, which did not amuse our landlady, but my mother laughed. She always let children be children and never took our small disobediences too seriously. Her sense of humor would not allow it.

Mentors are empathetic individuals who look out for other's best interests. They are nurturing and strive for the welfare of an individual. They are selfless and only want the best for those entrusted to their careful guidance. I can really say that my mother was my mentor. She was one of the only ones who offered individual attention to my growth and development, and it is because of this that her spiritual presence will be with me the rest of my life.

CHRISTIAN STEINER

JACK STERN

Rabbi Jack Stern was born in Cincinnati on July 27, 1926. He graduated with honors from the University of Cincinnati in 1948 and was then elected to Phi Beta Kappa. He then went on to the Hebrew Union College in Cincinnati, where he earned degrees as bachelor of Hebrew letters and master of Hebrew letters with honors. He was ordained at the college in 1952.

Rabbi Stern has been a vice president of the World Union for Progressive Judaism, a trustee of the Union of American Hebrew Congregations (UAHC), and president of the Westchester Board of Rabbis, the Scarsdale Clergy, and the Central Conference of American Rabbis (CCAR).

At present he is chairman of the task force on Jewish ethics for UAHC, member of the CCAR task force on human sexuality, and trustee of both Mazon and the Jewish Federation of the Berkshires.

WHEN I WAS A TEENAGER, I attended the Sunday morning religious school of my synagogue in Cincinnati. My teacher was Eugene Lipman, a student at the Hebrew Union College, on his way to becoming a rabbi. He was only seven years older than the pupils in our class, but he was still the teacher. He soon became a mentor and a friend, not only to me, but to anyone who would allow it to happen. As our mentor and friend, he let us know, without ever actually saying it, that he was continually available. He told us that he was there to listen; what a teenager needs more than anything is the world is for someone to be ready to listen.

Forty years later, Gene and I, now colleagues in the rabbinate, have remained close friends. Through all the years, my mentor-friend never stopped being my mentor-teacher. Simply to watch him, as a rabbi, as a human being, was constantly to learn.

He taught me that you cannot learn about life if you don't study the text of the Torah.

He taught me that justice, in order to deserve the name, had to be fair. Once, when I was serving on the ethics committee of our professional rabbinic organization, we were conducting a hearing on charges that a rabbi had violated standards of professional conduct. Suddenly, Gene Lipman showed up, uninvited, to take up the cause of the accused rabbi, not because he was convinced of his innocence, but because, according to Gene, the rest of us had denied that person due process. And he was right.

Gene taught me how to speak out, honestly and bluntly—though not always to the level of his own style of bluntness. He explained that I should let it be known when the emperor is wearing no clothes.

It all started in 1942, when Gene exerted a major influence on my decision, as a fifteen-year-old kid, to become a rabbi. Since then, for my forty years as a rabbi serving congregations, the powerful influence of the mentor has persisted.

Up until illness got the better of him, he would travel from his home in Chevy Chase, Maryland, to his one-and-a-quarter-acre vegetable garden in Dickerson, Maryland, where he tilled the soil and planted seeds. And when he harvested the crops, he would also take the tomatoes and carrots and beets to a house where there was hunger. The people in the house knew this rabbi only as the "vegetable man." Even until now, my mentor, friend, and teacher taught me to share what I have—and what I am.

I said these Hebrew words to him in person in his lifetime, and I say them to him now in his memory: *todah rabbah*—"great thanks."

Michael Strahan

Defensive end Michael Strahan has played for the New York Giants since 1993. He is a member of the 1997 Associated Press All-Pro Team, the 1997 Sports Illustrated All-Pro Team, the 1997 Pro Football Weekly All-NFL Team, the 1997 Pro Football All-NFC Team, the 1997 Sporting News All-Pro Team, and the 1997 NFC Pro Bowl Squad. He is a graduate of Texas Southern University.

Strahan is a spokesperson for HELP USA, a provider of homes, jobs, and services since 1986. He hosts homeless children at his football camp and conducts self-esteem workshops for youth in the New York City area.

MY FATHER WAS A MAJOR in the army and in 1981 we moved to Germany. I never played organized sports in Germany, but my father always kept me active there, taking me to work out in the gym or go fishing. He always stressed self-sufficiency and hard work. "You get out of life what you put into it," he would tell me. We would work out, and most of the time it was the last thing I wanted to do on a Sunday. I would have rather have been playing with my friends. "Keep working," my dad would say. "Someday this will all pay off."

It's almost as if my dad had a crystal ball; that he knew I would play professional sports.

In the beginning of my senior year in high school, Dad wanted me to return to the United States and try to get a football scholarship to a university. I thought he was crazy. I hadn't played football since I was eight years old. My father was very encouraging and made me feel that I was a better player than I actually was. He convinced me that I was capable, so I returned to the States and moved in with my dad's brother. I started playing football for Westbury High School and eventually did get a scholarship to Texas Southern University.

I wanted to quit during my first semester. I went back to Germany for Christmas holidays and brought everything from my dorm room with me. I even took my alarm clock. When it was time for me to return to school at the end of the holiday, I told my dad that I wasn't going back. He asked what I was going to do. I said that I wanted to stay in Germany and work with him at his transport company. He had since left the army and started his own business. After a slight pause he asked again what I was going to do. He made it very clear that working at his company was not an option. So I went back to school. Back at college, I realized that it was time for me to take all these lessons of self-sufficiency and hard work and put them to use. Three years later, after my senior year, I was drafted by the New York Giants.

The biggest influence for me in football was my first professional coach, Earl Leggett. Known as the Big Man, he was a former first-round draft pick himself.

Going into the game, I really didn't know all that much about football. In Germany, I had watched games on TV with my dad and read all the sports magazines. I knew enough about the game that, from the viewpoint of the defense, a quarterback sack was a good thing, and when I started playing in high school that's all I tried to do. I was big enough and fast enough to be a good player and naturally gifted enough to play football in college, but I had no technique. I had no sense of the strategy of the game. Thank God for Earl Leggett.

Coach Leggett taught me technique and showed how the repetition of drills and practice slowly became instinct, something performed almost unconsciously. He was an amazing teacher. He taught me to watch films of the other teams and to take notes critically. He showed me how to think like my opponents, how to anticipate their every move and adjust my game in the middle of the action accordingly. He explained the science of the game.

You have to be willing to learn, no matter how old you are. You have to get your ego out of the way, and being in the big leagues, you have to deal with a lot of ego. There are guys who feel that they are too big to learn or listen to anyone. As a result, everything becomes a conflict for them. It's sad. The coaches are only trying to make their team—*our* team—the best it can be, but some guys don't take it that way. To them it's all a personal insult because they aren't willing to admit that there are others who know a great deal more than they do. You go a lot further realizing that these people are here to help you and not to hurt you.

This applies to so many areas, not just football. In business, in school, in relationships, you've got to realize that you don't have the final answers, that you do need other people to help you out. And if you are open to that help, you'll be a lot happier and a lot more successful.

Three last bits of advice my father taught me: one, the best way to break a bad habit like drugs or alcohol is never start it; two, never ask someone to give you anything—always earn it first; three, if being successful was easy, everybody would do it, so you have to work hard for success.

COURTESY OF THE NEW YORK YANKEES

Joe Torre

Joe Torre enjoyed his finest season as a major league manager in 1998, guiding the New York Yankees to their second World Series championship in three years and establishing an American League record with 114 regular season victories. Including the postseason, the Yankees won a total of 125 games, breaking the major league record of 118 set by the 1906 Chicago Cubs.

As a player for the Atlanta Braves, St. Louis Cardinals, and New York Mets, Torre hit .297 in 2,209 games from 1960 to 1977, with 252 home runs and 1,185 runs batted in. A nine-time All-Star, Torre won the National League's 1971 Most Valuable Player Award after leading the league with a .363 batting average, 230 hits, 137 RBIs, and 352 total bases.

Primarily a catcher from 1960 to 1970, Torre spent his last seven seasons at first and third base.

Born and raised in Brooklyn, Torre is the first New York City native to manage the Yankees.

THERE ARE TWO INDIVIDUALS who have profoundly influenced my life: my older brother, Frank, and my wife, Ali.

I was the youngest of five children, all who were big baseball fans; I grew up surrounded by the game. Frank was more of a father figure than an older brother in that he paved my way through high school. He had also been a professional baseball player, so I guess you can say that he paved the road for me in my baseball career. He let me know what to expect and how hard I needed to work. Therefore, a compliment from him was worth more than anything. He was a tough taskmaster, but an inspiration nonetheless. There is a great difference in him now as compared to two years ago, before he had his heart transplant. Today he is traveling and active, his spirit revived and his passion for life thriving. Without his support and inspiration there would have been a large void in my life.

Baseball was a natural interest of Frank's, as it was with me. However, I was a New York Giants fan growing up, which was a dangerous thing to be living in Brooklyn. I was never a Yankees fan, yet I now have two World Series rings with the team.

The story goes like this: in November 1995 I was offered the manager's position with the Yankees; my daughter, Andrea, was born that December. Here I was at age 55 on the last few holes of an old golf course and another opportunity was about to open up for me. I have felt incredibly blessed and things have been nonstop wonderful ever since.

My wife, Ali, has also been a great source of inspiration and influence on my life in telling me to never give up my dreams. When I was fired from my manager's position with the Atlanta Braves in October 1984 she stood by my side and was always there for me. I remember watching a TV show with her and the theme was "How Do You Want to be Remembered?" Ali turned to me and asked that very question.

When I responded, "Someone who never accomplished what he wanted," she saw how down I was and kept my spirits up for the five or six years that I went into broadcasting.

During this time, I realized that when you are behind the mike for a while, you start to lose your competitive nature and forget how it feels to win; you lose the competitive nature of winning and losing. At that point in my career, and with that realization, having not won a World Series left me empty. Then, in 1990, I received a call from Dal Maxvill, a former teammate of mine and general manager of the St. Louis Cardinals. He offered me the position of manager and I stayed there until 1995, when I was fired early on in the season. Then Arthur Richman, a member of the Yankees organization who has been around baseball for nearly sixty years, called in November of that year and asked if I was interested in managing the Yankees. This was a welcome opportunity, albeit a surprising offer.

After the 1996 season, people were looking back and saying how much of that season was about my personal story, the personal battles in my life: my brother Rocco died in June and then Frank needed a heart transplant. The season was painted as a battle and then triumph for me. I was asked more than once: "Now that you've accomplished what you have wanted for so long, are you going to retire?"

"No," I said. "Why desert the coaches and players?"

Nineteen ninety-six was a magical year and I credit Ali with keeping my desire for baseball alive, my feet on the ground, and enabling me to return to coaching after broadcasting.

She was there for me again in 1997, when, after the first month of the season in early May, I wasn't having fun anymore. People only seemed occupied with getting another World Series win and asking me if that was all I wanted to accomplish, and now that I had that, what I was going to do. This preoccupation bothered me to the point that it caused me not to be happy and not to have fun. Ali pointed this out and said, "I don't know you anymore."

When I told her what was bothering me she said, "What do you care what people think?"

She was right. From that moment on I have never looked back. And life has been fantastic.

I also want to thank George Steinbrenner for allowing me the opportunity to win. He does this by signing good players and allowing me to reap the benefits of coaching them. You cannot win the Kentucky Derby with a quarterhorse, you need the caliber of a thoroughbred.

If you multiply what happened this year—the 1998 baseball season and our record 125 wins—tenfold, you will know how truly good things are.

Kathleen Kennedy Townsend

Kathleen Kennedy Townsend, Maryland's first lieutenant governor, has made it her mission to build safe communities across the state. She spearheaded the establishment of Operation Maryland Cease Fire and the Maryland Community Policing Academy. Since its inception in the summer of 1995, the unit has confiscated hundreds of assault weapons and other illegal firearms. She is also working to strengthen the juvenile justice and adult criminal justice system. While tough enforcement and punishment are essential, Mrs. Townsend strongly believes that prevention must be an equal priority. In addition, she has been a longtime advocate for children and families, serving as the chair of the state's Systems Reform Task Force for Children and Youth.

Mrs. Townsend is the eldest child of the late senator and U.S. attorney general Robert F. Kennedy. She is a cum laude graduate of Harvard University and a graduate of the University of New Mexico Law School.

THERE HAVE BEEN THREE PEOPLE whose wisdom and guidance most affected my perspective on the world and on my life. My aunt and godmother, Jean Kennedy, my law school professor Ruth Kovnat, and my dear friend Charlie Peters, the legendary editor of the *Washington Monthly.*

My Aunt Jean opened up the world of art, music, and theater for me. While I was growing up, my family had three very serious pursuits: politics, history, and sports. I thought that was what Kennedys did. My Aunt Jean revealed a different world. When I was sixteen, I began visiting her in New York and together we scoured the city for galleries and museums. She took me to concerts and plays—everything from Broadway shows to the avant-garde off-off-Broadway plays. She invited artists, musicians, actors, and writers to her home, turning it into a salon of sorts, where the most creative and exciting minds could come together to share their ideas. Even with all these people around her, Aunt Jean was interested in *my* life. When we were together, she asked me what I was reading at school and the ideas these works inspired in me. Our time together was fascinating and provocative. The ideas and arts she exposed me to offered entirely new perspectives on the world and doubled it in scope and richness.

Like most of the women of my generation, I didn't have any role models of what a woman could accomplish in the professional world. Women's involvement in public life was limited to volunteer or charity work. Even at Radcliffe, a woman's college, I didn't have a single woman professor. All this changed when I went to law school at the University of New Mexico, thanks to Ruth Kovnat. Ruth was a dazzling professor and one of the pioneers of environmental law. She came to New Mexico when her husband, a doctor, gave up his East Coast practice to work on an Indian reservation. We both lived in Santa Fe, so we rode together on the hour-and-a-half drive to school in Albuquerque. Talking for three hours a day, we became fast friends. We discussed law, the fascinating Indian cultures of New Mexico, and our families and careers. She invited me to her home for her family's Passover seder. Seeing her in her career as a professor and at home as a wife and mother was a revelation. Ruth showed me how a woman could fulfill her potential in the professional world while also being a wonderful wife and mother. This was extremely rare in the early 1970s, when the lack of role models forced many women into the false choice of either one or the other.

Ruth was living proof that a woman could excel professionally without abandoning the essential connections and relationships that fulfilled us as women. She gave me the confidence to pursue a career of my own.

After law school, I clerked for a federal judge and worked as an environmental lawyer, but never considered that I could pursue a career in politics. In 1980, I wrote an article for the *New York Times* on the importance of religious teachings to the principles of the Democratic party. Charles Peters, the legendary editor of the *Washington Monthly,* read it and asked me out to lunch to talk politics and ideology. Charlie had worked with my father and Uncle John on the 1960 presidential campaign, and later to create the Peace Corps, so we had a lot to talk about. We discovered that we shared many of the same political beliefs.

Charlie was the first person to suggest I run for political office. He told me that I had something to contribute to public life and could accomplish great things in politics. Even in the discouraging times after I lost the 1986 election to Congress, Charlie was steadfast in his encouragement. His faith in me buoyed me through tough times and convinced me to continue fighting in the political arena.

Aunt Jean, Ruth, and Charlie each remain a cherished friend, and our relationships have been strengthened throughout the years. I am deeply grateful for the instrumental role they have played in my intellectual, emotional, and professional growth. Each revealed to me new possibilities that I hadn't known existed. Aunt Jean taught me what was possible in art and beauty; Ruth Kovnat taught me what was possible in a woman's life; Charlie Peters taught me what was possible in my life. I am still learning and living what they taught me.

Stanley Tucci

Stanley Tucci's multiple talents have afforded him the opportunity to work with some of the best filmmakers of our time, and has joined their ranks. In 1996, *Big Night*, his first codirecting, coscreenwriting, and acting effort earned him numerous accolades. His second such project, *The Impostors*, which he starred in, wrote, directed, and coproduced, was an official selection at this year's Cannes Film Festival. He also recently completed playing Puck in the Michael Hoffman-directed adaptation of Shakespeare's *A Midsummer Night's Dream*.

Tucci recently played the role of Walter Winchell in the HBO original film *Winchell*. His last foray into television, Steven Bochco's *Murder One*, earned him an Emmy nomination for his role as Richard Cross. His other television appearances include episodes of *Equal Justice*, *Wiseguy*, *The Equalizer*, *thirtysomething*, and *The Street*.

On Broadway, he has appeared in numerous plays, including *Execution of Justice, The Iceman Cometh, Brighton Beach Memoirs*, and *The Misanthrope.*

IN MY SOPHOMORE YEAR of high school I auditioned for Gilbert Freeman, the drama and chorus teacher, with a comic skit that I had written. It was during the audition that I realized how at ease I felt onstage. Gil recognized this, and for the next three years instructed and encouraged me in the performing arts.

He always encouraged his students to take advantage of the city and its cultural life. Though not a professional actor or director himself, he more than understood the basic principles of acting and was very articulate in communicating them to high school students—not an easy task. To this day, I am thankful for his encouragement, and I make use of the simple but invaluable tools he gave me.

After high school I went to college at SUNY Purchase, an arts conservatory where I was fortunate enough to have George Morrison as my mentor. It was a very challenging and enormously freeing four years. But of all the myriad brilliant things George taught us, there is a single phrase or tenet that echoes everyday in my mind: "Go beyond what's comfortable." There are no more important words for any artist.

Of all the artists and teachers who have influenced me along the way, I would say that my father would rank first and foremost. He is both an artist and a teacher, having been the head of the art department at Horace Greeley High School in Chappaqua, New York. From the time I was four or five years old, I would accompany him to his summer school classes and the Saturday classes he taught throughout the year. As a teacher he had humor and patience, adapting himself easily to each student's needs, personality, and ability. Most important, he taught without judgment, believing that grades should not even be given in art. Effort was the only thing that he knew could be judged. It was for these reasons that I grew up not being afraid of my creative impulses, but following them.

This was not the norm for a boy growing up in a small town like Katonah, New York. In suburban America, boys are athletes and little more is expected of them other than good grades. But because both my parents encouraged creativity as well as athleticism and my dad had devoted his life to teaching art—and to the idea that creative expression and art in general was a necessity and not a luxury—I could not help but choose a life in the arts. It is a life that I am very proud of and hope that through my work I can instill the same feelings in others that he invoked in me.

To this day whenever I encounter my father's students, whether they are artists or not, they all remember him as one of the best teachers they ever had. I can only agree with them.

LILLIAN VERNON

Lillian Vernon is the founder and CEO of the Lillian Vernon Corp., a specialty catalogue company that markets gifts and household, gardening, decorative, and children's products.

Born in Germany, Lillian fled to the United States with her family before the onset of World War II and settled in New York City. She started her company in 1951 with a $2,000 wedding gift. She placed a $495 advertisement for a personalized purse and belt in *Seventeen* magazine and received $32,000 in orders; her business was launched.

Over the last forty-seven years, the company has experienced exceptional growth. Revenues for fiscal 1998 were $258 million. Last year the company received more than 4.9 million orders and employed over 4,700 people during its peak season.

Mentoring is a subject near and dear to my heart. When I started my business forty-seven years ago, I entered a world dominated by men, a world in which women, especially pregnant women, didn't work outside the home. At that time women really needed role models and mentors, but they were few and far between, except in businesses aimed at the female market. During the 1950s, professionals like Coco Chanel, Estee Lauder, and Elizabeth Arden, all pioneers in the fashion and cosmetics industries, were and still are prominent figures in business history. But where were the CEOs and presidents willing to take the time to help the next generation of professionals?

When I was seeking advice, counsel, and an occasional shoulder to lean on, I didn't even realize I was looking for a mentor. Fortunately, there were two people who *helped* me choose the path I ultimately took. I emphasize the word *helped* because, in my opinion, a mentor is someone who is willing to share their own experiences, recount their successes and mistakes, and offer opinions. A true mentor will never tell you what to do. Instead, they guide you, allowing you to make your own informed decisions.

Thomas Cochrane, one of my professors at New York University, served as an early mentor. Under his guidance, I learned the basics of clearheaded analysis and self-discipline, both of which proved to be invaluable in developing my business. I also owe a lot to my father, a successful businessman in his own right, who was one of my staunchest supporters. He gave me an education about business which encouraged and inspired me. He also gave me the best advice I could have received: "Persevere and never give up."

My father and Professor Cochrane inspired me to share my knowledge with many of my staff. Over the years I've mentored a number of men and women, many of whom now hold senior positions with the Lillian Vernon Corp. Acting as their mentor, guiding them to success in their career paths, has been one of the most personally and professionally fulfilling experiences that I've ever had.

Eli Wallach

Eli Wallach made his stage debut—and met his wife, Anne Jackson—in an off-Broadway production of Tennessee Williams's *This Property Is Condemned.* A leading interpreter of Williams's work, he has also appeared in *Camino Real* and *The Rose Tattoo,* for which he received a Tony and a Donaldson award. For his first film, *Baby Doll,* he won the English equivalent of the Academy Award in 1956. He has appeared in several Broadway and off-Broadway productions with his wife and has television credits that include *Rocket to the Moon, The Executioner's Song,* and *Anatomy of an Illness.*

Born in Brooklyn, he studied at the University of Texas and holds a master's degree in education from City College of New York. He began his training for the theater at the Neighborhood Playhouse and is a member of Actor's Studio. He loves tennis, photography, clock collecting, and architecture.

THERE WERE TWO PEOPLE who served as mentors to me as a young actor. The first was Sanford Meisner, a great acting teacher at the Neighborhood Playhouse School and Theatre. The other was Martha Graham, the brilliant teacher of dance technique and the Graham method at the playhouse.

Ms. Graham taught me that movement is a great tool—I use her teaching in every character I create on stage. Meisner also helped me by making me curious about the arts. "Read, read," he'd say. "Go to museums. Let the music enter your soul."

Both mentors stiffened my spine, told me I was unique. They said I should make voyages, attempt them—there's nothing else.

The impact of having older role models outside of my family was tremendous. Both pried open the doors of my mind. They were pioneers in their fields and great teachers, and they told me what I needed to hear: don't be disheartened, stay with your choice of career, and have the grit and courage to work, work, work.

For me as an actor, the turning point was my decision to stay with the theater. Television and film were temptations, but both Mr. Meisner and Ms. Graham taught me that as an artist I had to be tied to the live theater. Their lessons have stayed with me throughout my career.

Christine Todd Whitman

Christine Todd Whitman is New Jersey's first female governor and the first person to defeat an incumbent governor in a general election in modern state history. Taking office as New Jersey's fiftieth governor on January 18, 1994, she declared, "When one of us is out of work, homeless, cannot read, or is the victim of violent crime, we all suffer. And when we help one another succeed, we all succeed."

In 1995, she was the first governor chosen to give the formal response to a president's state of the union address, and served as honorary cochair of the 1996 Republican National Convention.

Governor Whitman is a former president of the New Jersey Board of Public Utilities and a former director of the Somerset County Board of Freeholders.

LOOKING BACK, I find it difficult to select just one person as my mentor. There are so many people who have helped me in my life and career. My parents, Webster and Eleanor Todd, were role models in every way. My brother, Dan, and my sister, Kate, have provided me with inspiration and advice throughout my life. And former New Jersey governor Tom Kean has always been there to guide me in my political career.

But outside my inner circle of family and friends there is one individual who had a profound impact at an important time in life—my student years at Wheaton College. That individual was Assistant Professor Daniel Lewin. He was a true mentor.

Professor Lewin's field of expertise was history and, in particular, Western European history. He was a scholar of the first degree who saw teaching as a profession of the highest order. He challenged his students, including me, to see history in new ways. He made history and international government come alive and poured his heart and soul into his chosen field.

I like to think that college is the one time in life when young people are most open to new ideas. I certainly was open to Professor Lewin's ideas. At a time when I was very unsure of my abilities, he gave me intellectual reinforcement by making learning easy. He also challenged me to think in ways I never had before, both academically and personally. He allowed me to participate in a senior seminar as a sophomore, which gave me the confidence I was lacking. And, he helped to shape my thinking on history and politics so much that I chose to major in history and international government.

At Wheaton, I became president of the Young Republicans, was vice president of my senior class, and graduated with honors in 1968. I think that Professor Lewin's mentoring played some part in all of my achievements at Wheaton and that each of these activities was an important stepping-stone in my career path.

Of course, it's difficult to say just how a mentor affects us, but I greatly respected Professor Lewin and miss him deeply. He died in 1967 from an overdose of medication he was taking to control epilepsy. Ironically, the day he died he was granted tenure as a full professor at Wheaton. He never knew that the college trustees had granted him this honor.

At the time of his death, Professor Lewin was just thirty-three years old. I will always remember attending his funeral and crying, along with so many others whom he had influenced. And I will always be impressed by just how much he was able to accomplish in just over three decades of life. He was a first-class scholar, a gifted teacher, a friend, and a true mentor.

JAMIE WYETH

STANLEY TRETICK

James Browning Wyeth received a public education only through the sixth grade and was then privately tutored. However, he holds honorary degrees from several schools: Elizabethtown College, the Dickinson School of Law, Pine Manor College, the University of Vermont, and Westbrook College.

Mr. Wyeth has had countless gallery exhibitions of his work. They include the M. Knoedler and Co. and Coe Kerr Galleries in New York City; the Pennsylvania Academy of Fine Arts in Philadelphia; the Anchorage Fine Arts Museum in Anchorage, Alaska; the Fitzwilliam Museum in Cambridge, England; and the Delaware Art Museum in Wilmington, Delaware.

In 1972, he was appointed a council member of the National Endowment for the Arts. Mr. Wyeth is a member of the board of governors of the National Space Institute, and belongs to the National Academy of Design and the American Watercolor Society. He has sketched Watergate incidents in the Senate and Supreme Court, and, in 1975, was a guest of the Soviet Union to tour the country's art centers.

LINCOLN KIRSTEIN WAS INTERESTED in my development as an artist and took it upon himself to help educate me. Since he was an art enthusiast and collector, he knew my father's works and was instrumental in buying *Christina's World* for the Museum of Modern Art. When I moved to New York at sixteen, he immersed me in learning. He taught me art history firsthand, taking me through all the museums and galleries in New York. He taught me architecture, business, history—he was an amazing trove of knowledge. Our friendship grew over the years until his death in 1996.

I remember walking with him through the medieval antiquities collection at the Metropolitan Museum of Art, pointing to a helmet and saying it reminded me of something from an Eisenstein film. He nodded his head and said that he admired the Russian filmmaker. A week later, I was visiting him at his house and relating the story of the medieval collection to a friend of his when Lincoln said that he had some "things" of Eisenstein's that might be of interest to me. These "things" turned out to be volumes of drawings and sketches by the filmmaker for his unfinished epic *Que Viva Mexico!* There were pages and pages of Eisenstein's storyboards for the film and sketches of planned film shots. Lincoln had received Eisenstein's sketchbooks as a token from the director for his substantial investment in the film. He had never mentioned this to me before. He was always very quiet about his "things." He didn't like his name attached to anything and preferred to stay out of the spotlight.

Lincoln was a remarkable philanthropist. He was responsible for the founding of the New York City Ballet and, along with the Rockefellers, was instrumental in the founding of the Museum of Modern Art. He was also a founder of Lincoln Center, and brought the famed Russian choreographer George Balanchine to the City Ballet.

He wore so many hats. He was a literary editor, an author, a painter, and a poet. But he had no ambition for a career as an artist. He had made up his mind at a very young age to give his life to philanthropy.

You had to self-educate yourself with Lincoln. He never said this is what you need to know; rather, he hinted at it and you had to find out about his hints. He made you make the discovery yourself.

I remember that I was fascinated with the dancer Rudolf Nureyev. I wanted to paint him but found Lincoln much against it. He said that Nureyev was a star—a grandstander who was not a company dancer—and being a "company dancer" was very much a part of Kirstein and Balanchine's vision for the New York City Ballet. Eventually I did paint Nureyev and exhibited this series. Lincoln saw the exhibit before it opened but did not comment on it. Later I learned that he had purchased one of the paintings.

Lincoln was a lone figure who didn't go to parties, premieres, or show openings. As he put it, he "wasn't housebroken." He always dressed in his own sort of uniform: a black suit, white shirt, and black tie. He was a big man with an even larger presence. When I first moved to New York, he promised that he would sit for a portrait for me. We scheduled a time for the drawing session and when I arrived at his door, I found him rushing out. "I've got no time right now, I have to go to this march in Mississippi!" Naturally, Lincoln was involved in the planning of the historic Selma civil rights march. He had simply forgotten to tell me about it and we had to reschedule.

Lincoln Kirstein was a mentor for many people. There's a stereotype of the kind and gentle teacher, but, typical of Lincoln, he was the opposite of what was accepted as the norm. He was not an easy man. He was very tough and extremely hard on me. But that was his way.

His influence on the arts in America has yet to be fully appreciated or understood. By arts, I'm not talking about specific disciplines such as dance or painting but the very concept of American art, as a whole, for the average person to be exposed to. Years from now, I think, he will be seen as a seminal figure for our times, not only for his monumental presence in American art, but also as a social activist and engineer.

In addition to the prominent Americans that appear in this book, two well-known British subjects, Sarah Ferguson, the Duchess of York, and Sir David Frost, write about their mentors.

SARAH FERGUSON

GORDON MUNRO

The Duchess of York, Sarah Ferguson, is the second daughter of Maj. Ronald Ferguson and his former wife, the late Mrs. Hector Barrantes. She married Prince Andrew, second son of Her Majesty, Queen Elizabeth II and the Duke of Edinburgh, at Westminster Abbey, on July 23, 1986.

The Duke and Duchess of York have two daughters. Princess Beatrice Elizabeth Mary was born on August 8, 1988, at the Portland Hospital, London, and Princess Eugenie Victoria Helena was born on March 23, 1990, at the same hospital. They are fifth and sixth in line of succession to the throne, respectively.

The Duchess founded Children in Crisis in 1993 and is chairwoman of the charity. Since its establishment, Children in Crisis has raised over $75 million to help children all over the world. It is one of the fastest growing charities in the United Kingdom. This expansion has led to the running of major projects in five counties.

WITHOUT QUESTION, my mother, Susan Barrantes, was my mentor. When she died tragically in a car crash, it was as if a light had gone out of my life. She was a unique person, and I lost a great friend as well as a fantastic mother.

People are sometimes curious about my relationship with my mother. We lived continents apart since I was barely a teen, yet the truth is that mum and I always had an uncommonly deep and unbreakable bond. Our love, trust, and mutual respect transcended distance and time because it was so pure and we remained intimate as a mother and daughter could ever be, right up to the time of her death.

Even as a young girl I recall my mother's simple, elegant beauty. She had a subtle yet dazzling presence, with an effortless style and an easy cleverness that drew people to her. But for me it was her gentle warmth and boundless energy that I adored most. Mum had a special way of making all things seem possible, and her positive outlook showed me a world that was brimming with color, excitement, and wonder. I suppose that's why I am always looking at the bigger picture in my own life, ever curious and prodding at boundaries to get at what's on the other side.

There was a private side to my mother that also had a tremendous influence on me. Mum was wise, incredibly strong, and full of kindness and compassion. I'll always be amazed by the way that this beautiful English woman followed her heart to a rural ranch in Argentina, where she knew little of the customs and did not speak the language. She was a stranger in a harsh and physically demanding land, but through her openness and caring ways, she was soon embraced by the entire community, and in many ways it was like an extended family to her.

I liken my mother to a winding river who encountered storms and hardship around every turn, yet flowed on with amazing strength and grace. By her example I learned to seize and savor the joys in my life, but it was also her absolute courage and dignity during her most difficult times that taught me the most about facing and surviving life's uncertainties.

DAVID FROST

Sir David Frost has not only won all major television awards, his professional activities have been so diverse that he has been described as "a one man conglomerate." Publisher, lecturer, impresario—Sir David Frost is ubiquitous.

Landmark interviews have always been the most prominent feature of Sir David's remarkable career. He has interviewed the six most recent presidents of the United States and the five most recent prime ministers of Britain. His interview of Richard Nixon was the most widely watched news interview in television history.

He garnered more attention for his outstanding PBS series . . . *Talking With David Frost,* which debuted in January 1991. Commenting on . . . *Talking With David Frost,* Rick Kogan of the *Chicago Tribune* wrote, "Few interviewers have been as constantly well-prepared, bright, and engaging as David Frost."

In January 1993, Sir David was knighted by Queen Elizabeth II. And in the fall of that year, the first volume of his memoirs, *David Frost: An Autobiography, Part 1—From Congregations to Audiences,* was published and became an immediate bestseller.

ONLY ONE PERSON COMES TO MIND who can be considered a mentor in my life—Geoff Cooksey. He was my English teacher from the time I turned fifteen until I was eighteen.

In 1956, I had just moved to a new school because my father was a minister and we traveled a lot. Mr. Cooksey was a remarkable human being whom I encountered at this very formative time of life. He ignited my interest in words as well as my passion for them. He made words irresistible to me.

One particular assignment comes to mind. Mr. Cooksey was concerned about the difference between a "loaded" article and an accurate one, between fiction and the truth. For that reason he told us to read two newspapers instead of one so we could learn to decipher this difference. We were taught to investigate in order to find the truth, and not to be afraid to question what was going on or what was being said.

When the 1956 war over the Suez Canal occurred, it caused great difficulty in England. England, France, and Israel attacked Egypt after its president, Gamal Nasser, nationalized the Suez Canal. Many people opposed the actions that were being taken. In fact, this was the beginning of a great division in England between those who supported the Suez actions and those who were opposed. At this time, Mr. Cooksey had us reading the *Observer,* a Sunday newspaper, so that we could keep informed of the current situation. We were urged to observe and to heed the great changes that were only just beginning to shape England at that time. This was occurring when it was still run by the "old school" style of rule—when leaders were more than adequately aware that they were still our, the students', elders and our betters, that their way of operating was best and proper. Also, about this time Mr. Cooksey took us to see a play by the brilliant playwright John Osborne. The play was called *Look Back in Anger* and it was staged at the Royal Court Theatre in London. The main character was a boy called Jimmy Porter, who originated the phrase "angry young man."

This play, and Mr. Cooksey, taught me to be more aware of the outside world, to observe the changes that were now going on in the country and to question the nature of things, particularly words. He also taught me how to relate what I was learning in English class, concerning literature and words, to the world around me. He explained that English is not just an important subject to which I must pay attention, but that the lessons I learned serve as paradigms for life experiences.

Mr. Cooksey gave me a new view of the future. He was an inspiring man who offered valuable lessons about the world. He taught me not to be afraid of change, but to confront it head-on and to look past an initial impression; to question the meaning of things and to learn from the changes those close observations can bring about. His teachings were instrumental because they inspired me to think for myself. He helped me to see the sheer pleasure in words and to learn from them. And he stimulated my mind. He was my mentor and my friend.